KEEP IT WORKING ... LONGER, BETTER!

Y0-ELD-737

2.~

2 —
SER

KEEP IT WORKING ... LONGER, BETTER!

A Practical, All-Purpose Household Reference

KATIE and GENE HAMILTON

ILLUSTRATIONS BY RAY SKIBINSKI

GUILDAMERICA BOOKS®

Doubleday Book & Music Clubs, Inc.
Garden City, New York

Text copyright © 1993 by A Perfect Partnership, Inc.
Illustrations copyright © 1993 by Doubleday Book & Music Clubs, Inc.
All Rights Reserved
Printed in the United States of America

ISBN: 1-56865-014-0

The Publisher and the authors have made every reasonable effort to ensure the accuracy and reliability of the information, instructions, and directions in this book. They disclaim any liability for misinterpretation of the directions, human error, typographical mistakes, or other loss or risk incurred as a consequence of the advice or information presented herein.

Book Design by Rhea Braunstein

ACKNOWLEDGMENTS

We'd like to thank all the service technicians and shop tenders at appliance and hardware stores who have answered our persistent nitpicking questions. During our research on how to make things work better we've met countless men and women who are experts in their field and have generously shared their knowledge with us.

We're indebted to our editor, Mary Sherwin Jatlow, who has extended her enthusiasm and helping hand and, of course, her editing expertise.

We're pleased to be working again with artist Ray Skibinski, whose clear and concise drawings illustrate this book.

And lastly, we're fortunate to have on our team Jane Jordan Browne, our agent and friend of many years, who not only coaxes and cajoles—she keeps us working!

We'd like to thank the following manufacturers and associations who helped us in researching the information for this book:

American Gas Assn.
Black & Decker, Home Products Div.
Black & Decker U.S. Power Tools Group
Certainteed Institute
Craftsman Tools; Sears, Roebuck and Co.
Electronic Industries Assn., Consumer
    Electronics Group
Eveready Battery Co.
Fieldcrest Mills
First Alert, Pittway
GTE's Sylvania Lighting Div.
Honeywell, Inc.
Lifesaver Smoke Alarms, Fyrnetics, Inc.
Mineral Insulation Manufacturers Assn.
Poulan/Weed Eater
Reflex, Heath/Zenith
Weber-Stephen Products Co.
Whirlpool
Wood Heating Education & Research
    Foundation

CONTENTS

If your house is anything like ours, it's filled with appliances, small machines, and specialized equipment that are just like the people who own and use them. They need tender loving care to keep them working.

Keep It Working . . . Longer, Better! tells you how to care for and maintain everything in your home. It's an A to Z guide with over 115 entries that include appliances, tools, home fixtures and furnishings, home electronics, outdoor equipment, and, of course, all the systems of a house that require regular maintenance to keep them running efficiently.

For each of the entries you'll learn what to do to avoid expensive service and repair charges. By following these quick-and-easy procedures you'll keep everything you own working at peak performance and running trouble-free. For example, a drop of oil in the right place can extend the life of an expensive appliance, and a simple chore like replacing a furnace filter will help the furnace run more efficiently and last longer.

Clearly drawn, user-friendly illustrations help you to better understand how and where to apply that drop of oil or where to find that furnace filter and how to replace it.

We know you lead a busy life, so the maintenance routines are not time-consuming, tedious chores or heavy-duty repairs—they're "minute maintenance" tips, the minimum requirements for better operation. These are things you'll actually do because they're so simple.

Since the maintenance procedures are doable and simple, they require only basic tools. You probably already own most of the tools, but in case you're a new homeowner and just beginning to maintain your house, you'll find a complete list of tools you need to complete the tasks in this book.

All oils are not created equal, so a list of lubricants will help you purchase the right products to keep everything in your house humming along.

To help in overall planning there's a "Homeowner's Seasonal Checklist" with suggested tune-up tips during the year, which will help you to set up your own household maintenance schedule.

This book isn't meant to replace all your owner's manuals—they are a valuable source of information—but if you can't find them, you won't go wrong following the suggestions in *Keep It Working . . . Longer, Better!*

SAFETY FIRST

While you're tinkering with things around the house, don't forget about playing it safe, even for the easiest of tasks. Give yourself more than enough time to complete a job so that you're not rushed or pressured to take shortcuts that might cause an accident.

Before beginning a task, assemble all the materials and tools you'll need so that you won't have to stop in the middle. The simple maintenance projects in this book require only a basic tool kit, so purchase the best quality tools you can afford. Quality tools last a lifetime and are safer to use because they are well designed and made of long-lasting materials.

Dress for success—the job at hand. Don't wear loose clothing that can get caught in machinery. The maintenance in this book does not require strong solvents, but since detergents can be hard on your hands, wear a pair of household rubber gloves as a precaution. When you're working on anything with sharp metal parts (i.e. an air conditioner), protect your hands by wearing a pair of work gloves.

If you are hammering or striking any two steel tools together, be sure to wear safety goggles. They also help keep dust and dirt from getting into your eyes when you are vacuuming or blowing dirt out of appliances.

When working on an electrical appliance, unplug it and shut off the power to the entire area at the main service panel in your home. Don't rely on the "on" and "off" switch on the wall because someone might walk in and flick the switch by accident.

Use a solid surface to do your maintenance. If you're working on a small object that's difficult to see, bring in an extra light. Make sure that your work area has plenty of ventilation if you are using solvents or cleaners that give off fumes.

Before climbing a ladder, make sure that it's sturdy, without any loose or rotten rungs or rails. Never extend the ladder to its full length or stand on the very top rung. Always move the ladder close to your work so that you don't have to reach out a far distance to either side. Also, if you are working on a ladder or roof, wear soft rubber soled shoes for safe footing.

TOOLS AND SUPPLIES

The well-stocked tune-up tool box includes:

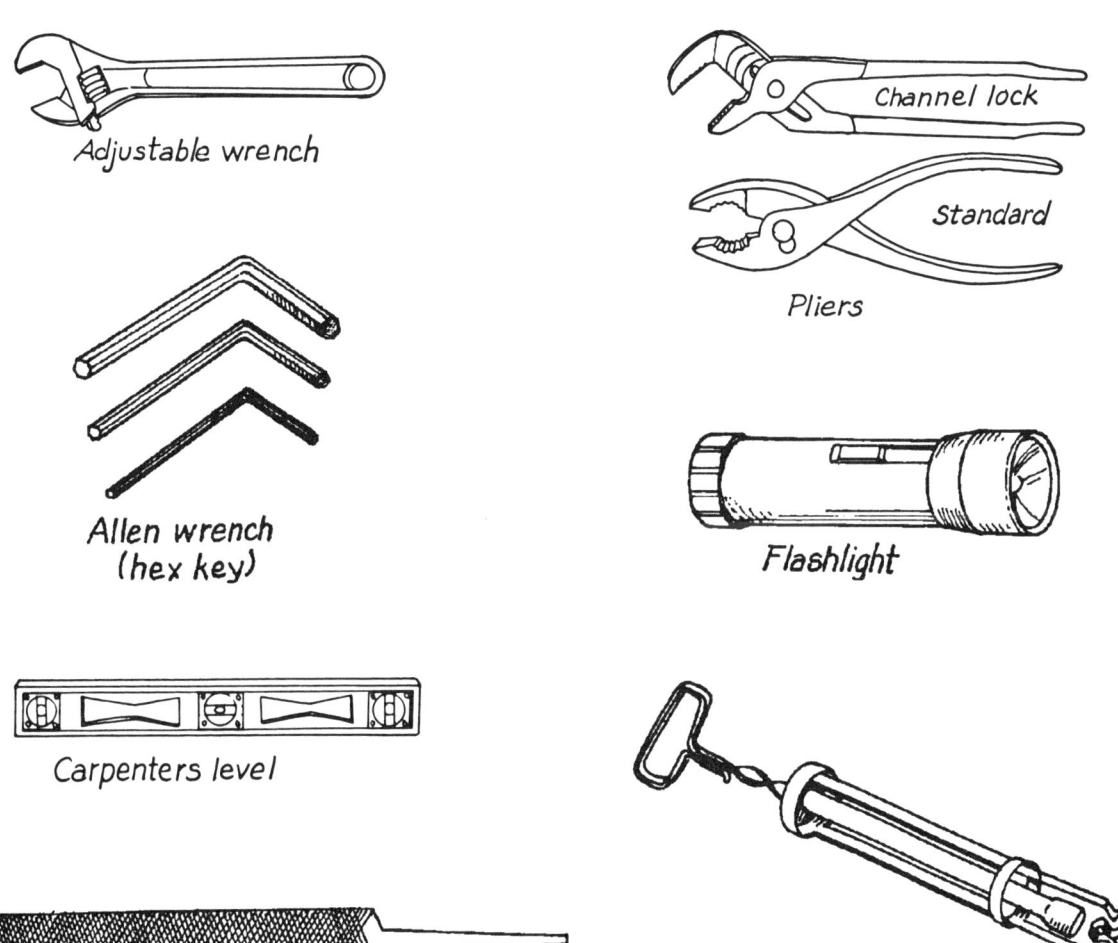

Adjustable wrench

Channel lock

Standard

Pliers

Allen wrench
(hex key)

Flashlight

Carpenters level

File

Paintbrush spinner

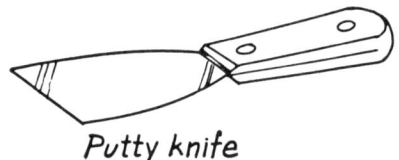

Putty knife

Sawhorse

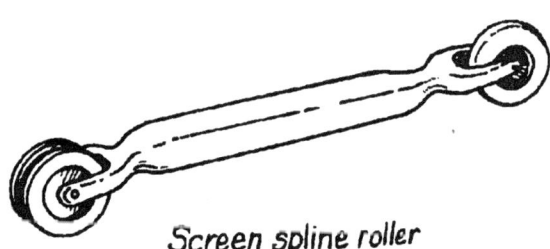

Screen spline roller

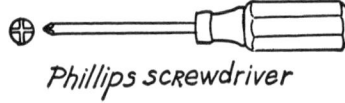

Phillips screwdriver

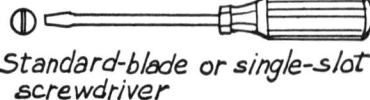

Standard-blade or single-slot
screwdriver

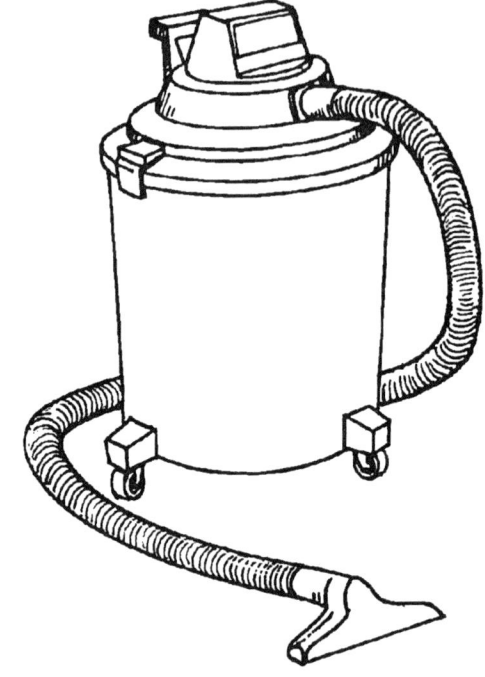

Shop vacuum

Utility knife

Wire brush

SPECIALTY TOOLS:

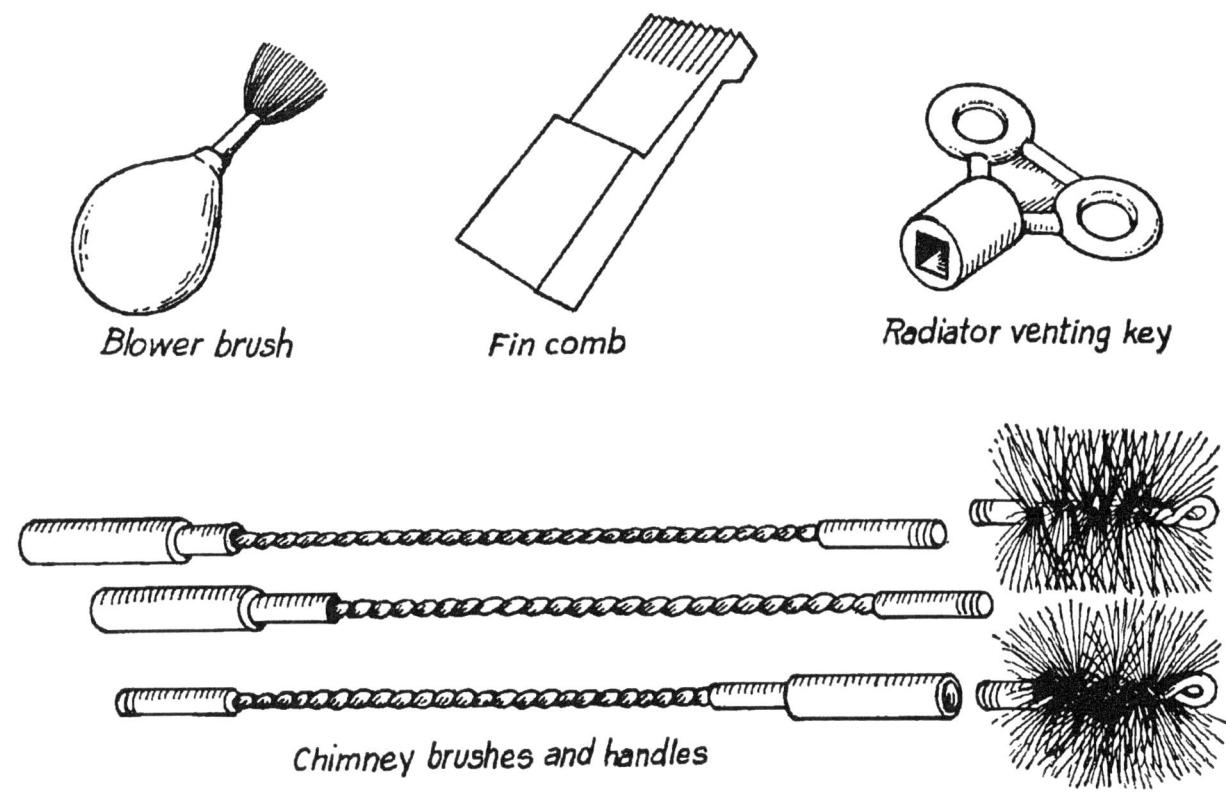

Blower brush   Fin comb   Radiator venting key

Chimney brushes and handles

LUBRICANTS:

Household Oil: 3-in-one® is a small red, white, and black can of lightweight lubricating oil used to loosen rusted parts and to be applied anywhere a light easing oil is needed.

Motor Oil: This light 20- and 30-weight fluid lubricant is used to reduce friction in areas like bearings, hinges, and other places that rub together. 3-in-one® brand motor oil is a widely available SAE (Society of Automotive Engineers) 20-weight oil suitable for most applications, including lubricating the bearings of 1/4 horsepower and larger electric motors.

Penetrating Oil: The two most popular brands are WD-40® and Liquid Wrench®. These oils are used to loosen a bolt that is "frozen" or rusted in place, to free sticky mechanisms, and to stop squeaks.

These lubricants come in an aerosol can with a thin straw that attaches to the nozzle head to direct the oil into small, difficult-to-reach places.

Silicone: This dry lubricant, which is available in a spray can or in a stick-like crayon, is used to reduce friction between parts that rub or slide together. It is especially useful in areas where standard oil attracts dirt.

Special Purpose Oils: There are several oils developed to lubricate a specific item. These include sewing machine oil, lawn mower and power equipment oil, and bicycle oil.

White Lithium Grease: This multipurpose lubricant, sold in a tube or an aerosol spray, keeps metal parts working smoothly and prevents the buildup of dirt and rust.

HOMEOWNER'S SEASONAL CHECKLIST
TO KEEP THINGS WORKING

SPRING

tune up air conditioner
clean outdoor wood deck /
    fix protruding nail heads
clean gutters and downspouts
clean fireplace / wood stove
tune up humidifier
check sump pump
clean and check awnings
wash/hang door and window screens
check battery in smoke detector

SUMMER

coat asphalt driveway
tune up dehumidifier
drain hot water heater
change or clean filters in air conditioner
wash aluminum or vinyl siding
clean barbecue grill
service garage door opener
cut back shrubs around heat pump/
    air conditioner
clean ceiling fan

FALL

clean chimney
check boiler, furnace, and heat pump
drain radiators
check thermostat
wrap window air conditioner
check weather stripping
wrap water pipes
clean gutters and downspouts
turn off outdoor water supply
winterize outdoor equipment
check battery in smoke detector
hang storm windows and door

WINTER

drain hot water heater
change furnace filters
tune up humidifier
check water softener
clean range hood filter
clean and service house, exhaust,
    and window fans

KEEP IT WORKING ... LONGER, BETTER!

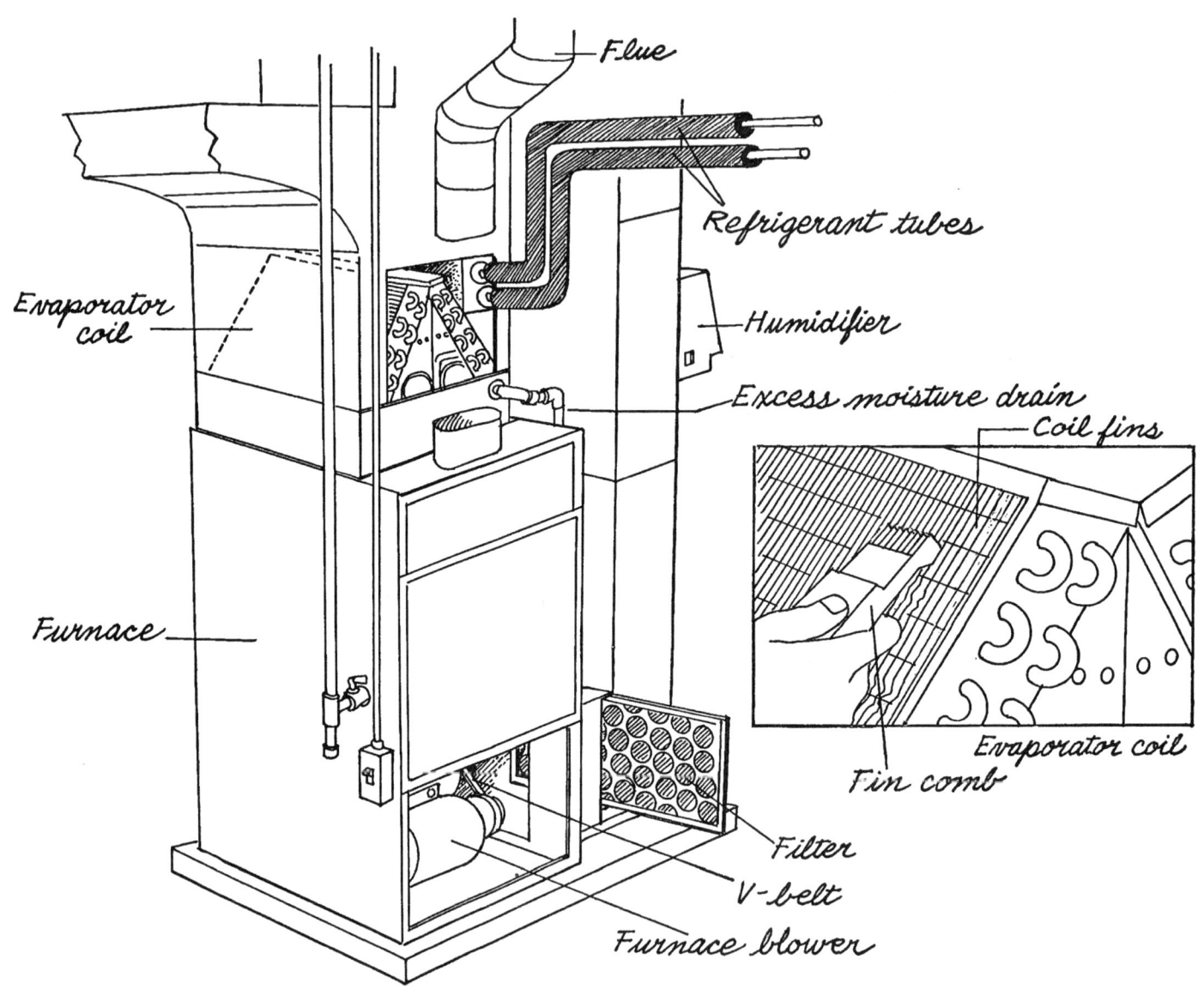

Flue

Refrigerant tubes

Evaporator coil

Humidifier

Excess moisture drain

Coil fins

Furnace

Evaporator coil

Fin comb

Filter

V-belt

Furnace blower

AIR CONDITIONER, Central

Central air conditioner units run trouble-free most of the time. Periodic professional maintenance to check the compressor and refrigerant levels will help you realize the most cooling for your energy dollars. There are, however, several simple tasks that you can perform that will extend the life of the unit and keep it working efficiently.

Most central air conditioners distribute cool air through a house with the same air handling system that the heating system uses. The air conditioner uses the furnace motor and blower so it is pulling air through the furnace filter whether it is cooling or heating. To get the most out of the air conditioner, change your furnace filter regularly, even during the summer.

If a house has radiators or baseboard heat, the air conditioner blower unit will be separate from the boiler. It may be located in the basement but more likely it will be in the attic. The blower unit has the same basic components as a forced air furnace equipped with central air conditioning and is serviced in the same way. Before you begin any work on your air conditioner, turn off the power to both the air conditioner and the furnace at the main power panel in your house.

Replace or clean the air filter *at least once a month.* This filter is usually located in the base of the furnace in the return air duct. Dirty handprints on the side of the furnace or air conditioner blower unit left by a previous owner or serviceman are a good tip-off to the filter's location. If you can't find it, consult your owner's manual.

If your furnace has a permanent filter, a frame with a washable foam filter stretched over it, remove and wash the filter in warm water and a mild detergent. Then allow it to dry on a flat surface before reinstalling it on the frame.

If your furnace has a fiberglass filter in a paper frame, discard it after it fills with dirt. Measure this filter or read the size marked on the frame and buy a couple of replacement filters. It's a good idea to keep your eyes open for "filter sales" and always have a supply on hand.

At least once a season, preferably before the air conditioner is turned on, clean the evaporator coil (triangular in shape and usually located in the top of the furnace in the main duct). It is usually accessible through an inspection cover on the side of the furnace. Use the crevice tool of a vacuum to suck up the dirt and dust lodged between the coil fins.

To blow loose dirt and lint from the coil fins, reverse the hose on the vacuum so that it blows outward or use a hair dryer. Aim the hose or hair dryer at the outside of the coil to dislodge the particles that have been blown into the coil from underneath. Straighten any bent fins with a fin comb or use the blade of a small screwdriver; be careful not to damage the core tubing.

On humid days this cold coil will condense a lot of water from the air, so check that the drain line serving the drip pan under the evaporator coil is not clogged. Also clean the drip pan carefully so the drain will not clog up later in the season. When everything is clean, replace the inspection cover.

Keep the area around the air conditioner's outdoor condenser clean. Trim back any bushes or weeds that grow around the unit so nothing obstructs the passage of air through it.

AIR CONDITIONER, Window unit

Keeping the filter of a room air conditioner clean is the key to having an efficient, long-running unit. During the cooling season, when it's working full-time, check the filter **at least once a month** and wash it whenever it appears dirty.

Turn the air conditioner off and unplug it before you work on the unit. The filter is located behind the front grill. To remove it, open the front of the unit. Getting the grill open can sometimes be a puzzle: Some are hinged and snap open when you pull on the top or bottom; others come completely off if you lift them slightly. If you are unable to get the air conditioner's grill to budge, take your time in figuring out how it is held in place. Don't pull or pry it because you might break the hinges or plastic tabs that hold it in place.

Behind the grill you'll find a foam filter. It is usually hung or draped over a plastic frame or it rests on small protruding tabs that keep it in place. The filter is thin and flimsy and can tear easily, so work carefully as you remove it. Sheets of filter foam can be purchased at most hardware stores and home centers. If the filter is brittle or crumbly, don't bother trying to clean it. Purchase a replacement filter and cut it to size.

If the filter is in good condition, shake out any loose dust and dirt. Remove the heavy dirt from the filter with the upholstery tool of a vacuum. With most of the heavy dirt removed, wash the filter in warm water and mild detergent. Rinse it in clear water and then let it dry flat to maintain its shape.

While the filter is removed, you have access to the evaporator coils which are directly behind the filter. Use the crevice tool or brush of a vacuum to suck out dust and dirt that accumulate around the coils. Be careful not to bend the soft aluminum fins

with the crevice tool and try not to push the dirt deeper into the coils. You'll find that it's easiest to clean the evaporator coil when the unit is dry.

Air must pass between the coil fins to become cool, so if they are badly bent, the unit will be very inefficient. If the coil fins are bent or misshapen, push them gently back into position with a thin object such as a craft stick or a putty knife. For badly bent fins, purchase a fin comb at a local appliance store or air conditioning retailer. A fin comb looks like a hair comb and has teeth the exact width of the coil fins, so passing it through bent coils straightens them for better air passage.

An air conditioner works best if it is level or tipped slightly so the side of the unit outside the window is lower than that inside. This promotes proper drainage. Use a carpenter's level placed on the top of the unit to see that it is even. If it isn't, place a shim (a piece of wood shingle sold at lumberyards) under the low side to raise it.

Check the weather stripping around the unit and window **once a year.** Give special attention to the foam strip between the outer and inner window sash. Foam ages quickly and becomes stiff when it is exposed to the sun. If the strip is more than a couple of years old, replace it with a new piece. Check to see that the side curtains of its frame fit snugly and recaulk any open seams between the frame and the window jamb.

If the unit is easy to work on, clean the condenser coils at the back of the unit. If you see debris around the coils, use a vacuum's crevice tool to remove it.

Check that the condensation drain located in the bottom of the unit is open. On a humid day, water dripping from the evaporator coils can back up

2

inside the bottom pan of the unit and eventually leak into the house. Check to see that this drain is clear and that nothing blocks it.

Inspect the area outside the window. Trim back overgrown shrubs or tree branches that block the passage of air around the unit.

If you store the unit in place in the winter, cover it with an insulated cover. If you remove it from the window, cover and store it in a dry location. If it was stored tilted or on end, allow the unit to sit in the window for several hours before you start it so that the lubrication can settle in the compressor.

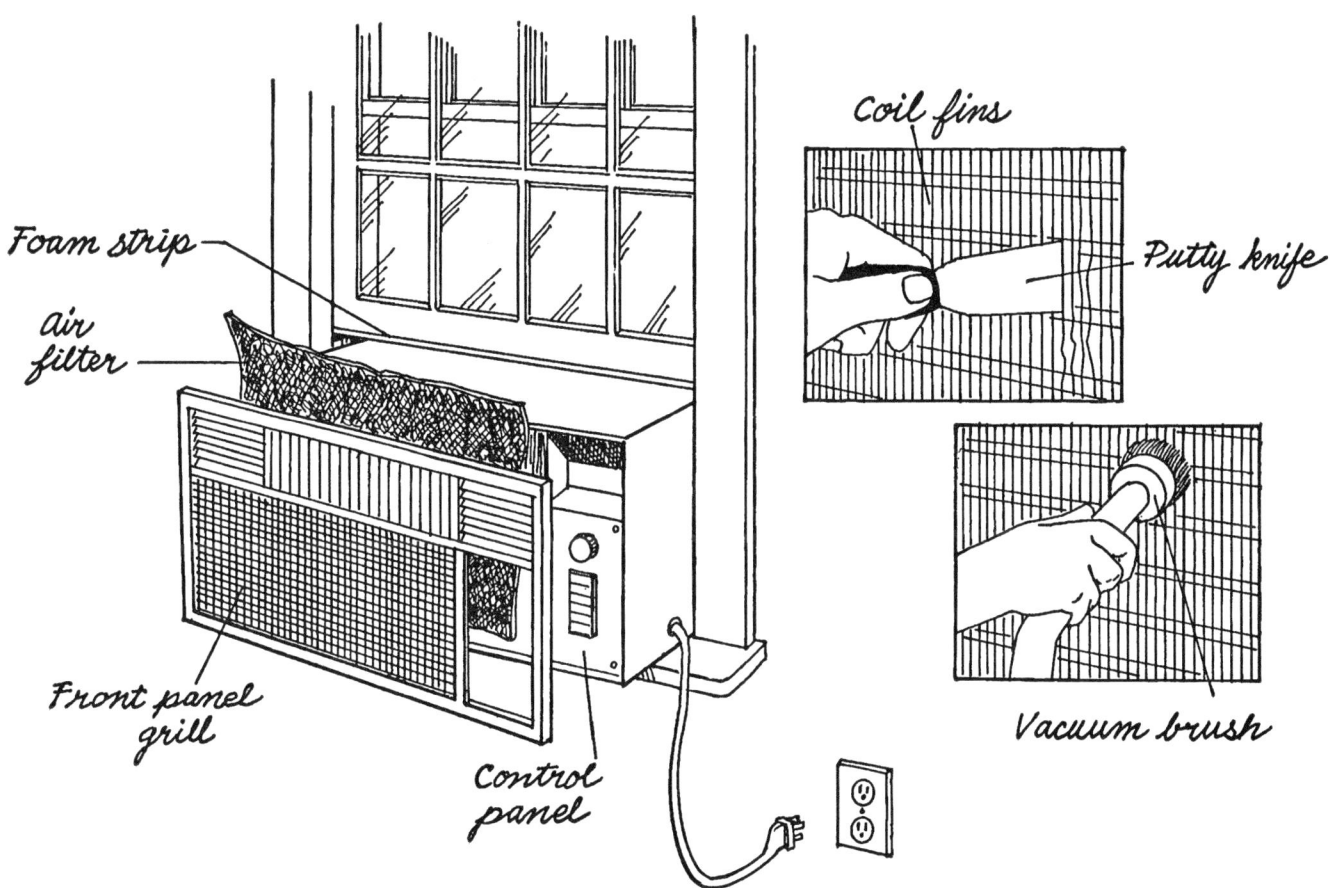

Foam strip

air filter

Front panel grill

Control panel

Coil fins

Putty knife

Vacuum brush

ALUMINUM SIDING

Aluminum siding is advertised as maintenance-free and for the most part it is. A *yearly* rinsing with a hose will keep it clean. Clean damp, shaded areas where mildew develops with a solution of water and an all-purpose cleaner with disinfectants. Apply it from a bucket with a sponge or rag mop and rinse the area thoroughly with plenty of water.

Scuff marks and stubborn dirt can be scrubbed away with a mild abrasive cleaner. An inexpensive nonpolluting cleaner is borax powder. Wet a sponge and wring it out so that it's damp. Then dip the sponge into borax powder and use it like a scouring pad. Rinse the area thoroughly with water.

Inspect the siding for open seams where caulking has weathered and begun to crack or pull away. Carefully check the joints over each window because water gathered in the top molding can run behind the siding if the joint is not properly sealed. Remove any bad caulk and replace it with a top-quality latex caulk containing silicone.

ANTENNA

A television antenna is one of the few pieces of equipment around a house that is almost totally maintenance-free. About all you can do to keep it working is to cut back any tree branches nearby so they don't damage it. If part of the antenna gets bent, straighten it out carefully because the lightweight tubing breaks easily once it is kinked.

Once a year, or more frequently if you live in a high wind area, make an inspection of the mounting bolts that hold the antenna to the chimney straps or to the roof. See that they are tightened securely. Wind vibration can loosen the bolts and in time, if they become loose, the antenna will sway in a strong wind, causing the mounting system to break eventually. Check that all guide wires are secure.

Also, make sure that the lead-in cable is securely fastened to the house. If it becomes loose and is allowed to bang against the house, it will chafe and eventually fail, not to mention marring your home's siding.

AQUARIUM

Keep in mind that any maintenance activities in the tank are disturbing to the fish, so plan your moves carefully.

Once a week, exchange about one fourth of the old water in the tank with an equal amount of fresh tap water of the same temperature. Use a siphon to transfer the old water into a bucket. Check to see that all filters are clean, with water flowing through them, and that all hoses are connected and functioning properly.

Check the aquarium for dead or overgrown plant leaves. Use your hands to pinch off any dead leaves and snip off any large leaves that shield other plants from light. Thin out floating plants like duckweed so that they do not become overbearing.

ASPHALT DRIVEWAY

Gardening or "weeding" is the first step to keep an asphalt driveway or walkway in good condition. Maintain the ground surrounding the asphalt so that it's free of weeds and keep the grass cut close to the ground along the driveway edges. If cracks or crevices occur in the asphalt, pull out pesky weeds before patching them.

Park your car in different spots of an asphalt driveway to avoid spotting it with water and oil drip marks. Remove oil spots with an asphalt cleaner. Gas leaking from your car can be harmful to both the car and the driveway because it eats into the asphalt and begins to melt it. If you notice that a soft spot in the driveway is developing under the car, have a mechanic check your car for a gas leak immediately.

Once every two years, patch minor cracks or holes and then reseal the surface. This will extend the life of an asphalt driveway or walkway almost indefinitely. You can hire a driveway sealing contractor to do this messy job or you can do it yourself.

Water-based driveway sealers, sold in 5-gallon buckets, are the easiest to use. Small cracks should be filled with driveway sealer or asphalt sealing caulk sold in standard 10.5-ounce caulk tubes. You can also fill small cracks with a mixture of sand and driveway sealer. *(Illustration, p.6.)*

Choose a warm day with a rain-free forecast for the next few days. Sweep all leaves and dirt from the driveway and then patch the cracks. When they're dry and hardened, pour sealer onto the driveway surface and spread it with an old push broom or squeegee. Two thin applications of sealer are better than a single thick one. Block off the driveway with the empty cans so that no one will drive on it for a few days.

CARE OF AN ASPHALT DRIVE

Trim back grass and weeds.

Push broom

Sealer

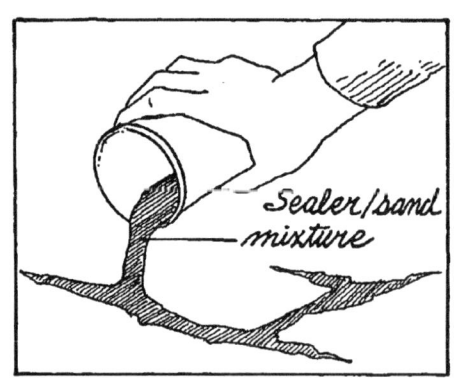

Sealer/sand mixture

Fill small cracks with sealer.

Fill large cracks with asphalt pitch.

ATTIC INSULATION

All types of attic insulation are designed to be maintenance-free. Insulation loses its effectiveness if it gets wet or is packed down. When working with insulation, wear a respirator to protect your lungs from inhaling dust particles and an old long-sleeved shirt and long pants. If you don't have a respirator, you should at least use a dust mask.

If a roof leak develops and the attic insulation becomes wet, don't let it lie on top of a plaster or drywall ceiling because the insulation traps moisture and prevents the ceiling from drying out. This causes stains and eventual delamination of the plaster or drywall. Remove wet insulation as quickly as possible to start the drying-out process.

If the insulation is loose-fill cellulose or chopped fiberglass, scoop it up with a small shovel or dustpan and spread it around on top of the dry insulation. Remove wet fiberglass-type insulation by pulling it up from between the floor joists. Roll or faced insulation can be removed by pulling each piece along its side to tear the facing where it is stapled to the ceiling joist. When the insulation and ceiling have dried for at least a week, replace the insulation. Fluff up any loose fill and you can expect to receive its full insulating value.

Sometimes loose-fill insulation becomes compacted tightly between the ceiling joists because of heavy boxes stored on top of it for long periods of time. If that happens, use a stick to fluff it up in order to match the height of the other insulation in the attic.

AWNING, Aluminum

Rigid aluminum awnings have a durable painted surface created to withstand most weather conditions. The finish will eventually become oxidized by the weather and begin to chalk, but by washing your awnings *once a year* with a household detergent, you will postpone the process, especially in urban areas where accumulated dirt from the atmosphere contains industrial pollutants and acids.

Also inspect the screws or bolts that hold the awning to the window frame or siding. An awning may be made of lightweight aluminum sheeting but it will stand up to high winds as long as the awning stays firmly attached to the building. If a corner of

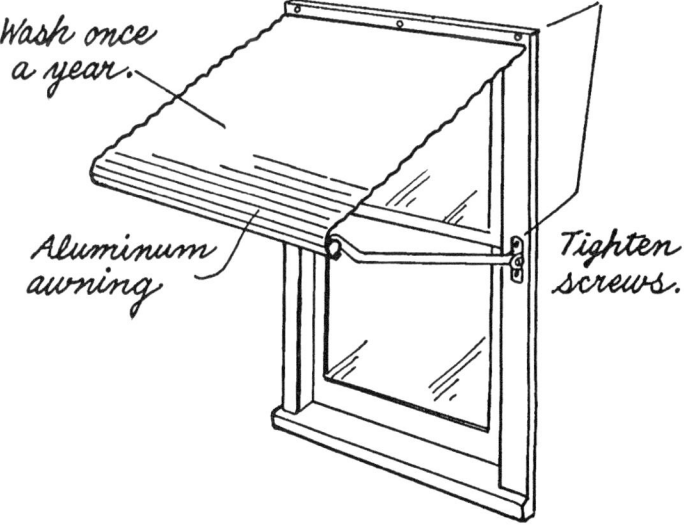

Wash once a year.

Aluminum awning

Tighten screws.

the awning works loose, the entire awning is in danger of being bent or ripped off.

Tighten any loose wood screws *(see "Awning, Canvas")* and repair any screws that have worked themselves loose. You can replace a loose screw with one that is one size larger and slightly longer because it fills the oversized hole and tightens in it securely. Use only brass- or zinc-coated screws to prevent rusting.

AWNING, Canvas

Inspect and clean canvas awnings **once a year.** Check to see that the metal frame which holds the awning to the house is securely fastened. High winds can shake the frame and loosen some of its screws, which will pull out and tear the awning.

Tighten all loose screws and bolts on the frame. Look closely at the bolts that attach the awning to the house brackets. Tighten these or replace them if they are bent.

If you find loose wood screws in the brackets holding the awning to the siding or window trim, remove the loose screws from their holes. Then dip the shaft of a wooden match into glue and push it into the enlarged screw hole. Break the match off flush with the bracket and then reinstall the screw.

Look for signs of wear and tear on the canvas fabric. The canvas is typically reinforced at its corners and where friction will cause it to wear thin. Using a heavy-duty needle, restitch any loose threads or have the canvas repaired by a professional.

Clean the awning when it gets dirty. If it's retractable, unroll it so that it is in an extended position. Use a soft brush and a solution of mild soap and water to thoroughly wash the canvas fabric. Let it dry completely in its extended position.

To remove mildew and stained areas, use a

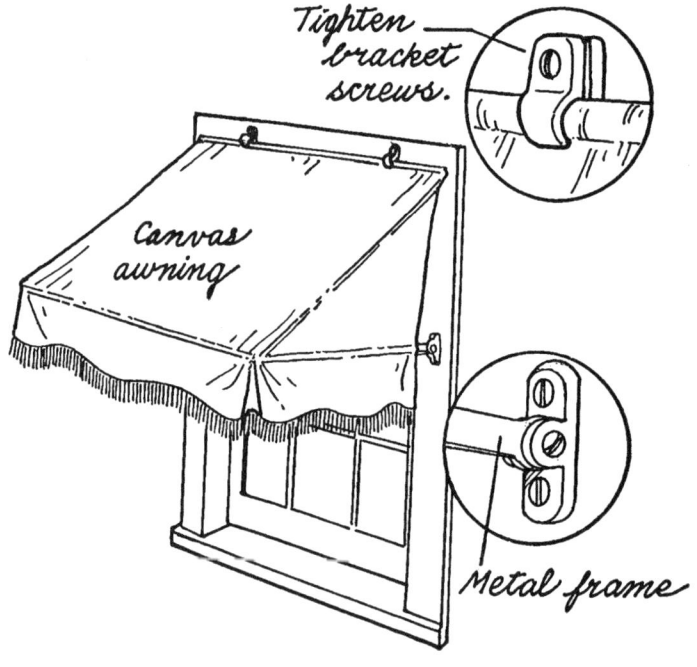

brush dipped in a paste made of washing soda and water. Continued rubbing is usually required to remove persistent stains.

In severe winter climates, canvas awnings should be removed from their frames and stored indoors so that heavy snowfall doesn't damage them.

BARBECUE GRILL, Charcoal

When it's not being used, store a covered grill with all of its exposed vents closed to keep rainwater from getting inside and rusting interior surfaces. Store an open grill by keeping it out of the sun and rain and protecting it with a heavy plastic garbage bag or similar covering. Loosely tie a string or shock cord around the plastic to keep it secure.

Before you use a grill, make cleanup easier by applying a nonstick vegetable cooking spray, e.g. Pam®. The best time to clean a grill is when it's still hot after food preparation. Use a grill brush, which is a combination scraper and wire brush, to handle the job quickly and easily; or a pair of tongs, holding a wad of aluminum foil used as a scraper, to scrub off encrusted food.

If food has dried and hardened on the grill, apply a spray-on oven cleaner following the directions on its label, or soak the grill overnight in a washtub filled with hot water and dishwashing detergent.

If a grill is not in use during the winter, remove any ashes and old charcoal briquettes because they hold moisture and promote rusting.

Inspect the outside of the grill for chipped paint. Where there's a chip, use a piece of 120-grit abrasive paper to sand the area smooth until the metal is clean and all rust is removed. Then recoat the sanded area with a high-temperature paint, which is available in spray cans at most paint stores, large home centers, and lumberyards. Black paint is readily available. For other colored barbecue kettles or grills, contact the manufacturer to see if they sell a paint touch-up kit in the color needed. It usually comes in a small bottle (like nail polish) or a spray can, so it's easy to apply.

Wooden handles and trim that are not severely weathered should be lightly sanded and then given a coat of a wipe-on oil finish. If the finish has worn away or the wood is gray, dry, and checked, paint it instead of trying to refinish it.

To paint the handles, sand the wood lightly and apply two or three coats of exterior house paint, which will stand up to the weather and be more maintenance-free than a clear finish.

BARBECUE GRILL, Gas

Basic maintenance for a gas grill is the same as for a charcoal grill. In addition to a good cleaning, the gas burner and LP gas tank should also be cleaned **once a year.**

To clean a gas barbecue grill, put a large piece of heavy-weight aluminum foil (shiny side down) on top of the grill, leaving gaps on the sides open. Ignite the grill, turn burners to a high setting, and with the lid closed let it run for 10 minutes. Turn all the burners to "off" and let the barbecue cool. Crumple the aluminum foil into a wad and use it to brush off any ashes or food particles. Before cleaning the bottom tray and catch pan, turn the gas grill off and wait for it to cool down. Then use a brass bristle brush (barbecue grill brush) and wash with warm soapy water.

BARBECUE-Gas

Clean tank.

Sand lightly and apply oil finish.

Periodically throughout the season, make a spider and insect inspection in the burner tubes of the grill. Spiders and other insects like to nest in the confines of the burner tubes. Their webs or cocoons block the air-gas mixture from getting through to the burners. Make this inspection if any of the following conditions occur: there's a smell of gas with burner flames that appear very yellow; the barbecue doesn't reach cooking temperature; it heats unevenly; or the burners make popping noises.

Barbecue gas grills vary according to manufacturers. Here's a basic outline of how to inspect and clean burner tubes:

- Turn off the gas and allow the unit to cool.
- Remove the control knobs (most pull off).
- Remove the control panel, if necessary.
- Look inside the burner tubes for insects or dirt (use a flashlight if necessary).
- Clean the inside of the burner tubes. Remove burnt food particles from the small holes around the outside of the burner with a stiff brush or burner cleaning tool.
- Remove cobwebs or dirt from the air shutter.
- Reassemble the unit in reverse order.

During the off-season when the grill is not in use, store the grill in a well-ventilated area (preferably outside in a storage shed or in the garage). If you can't store the unit outside, disconnect the LP tank and store it separately. Don't store the LP tank or barbecue with the tank attached in a confined area because even a very small gas leak can accumulate in an unvented area and become an explosion hazard.

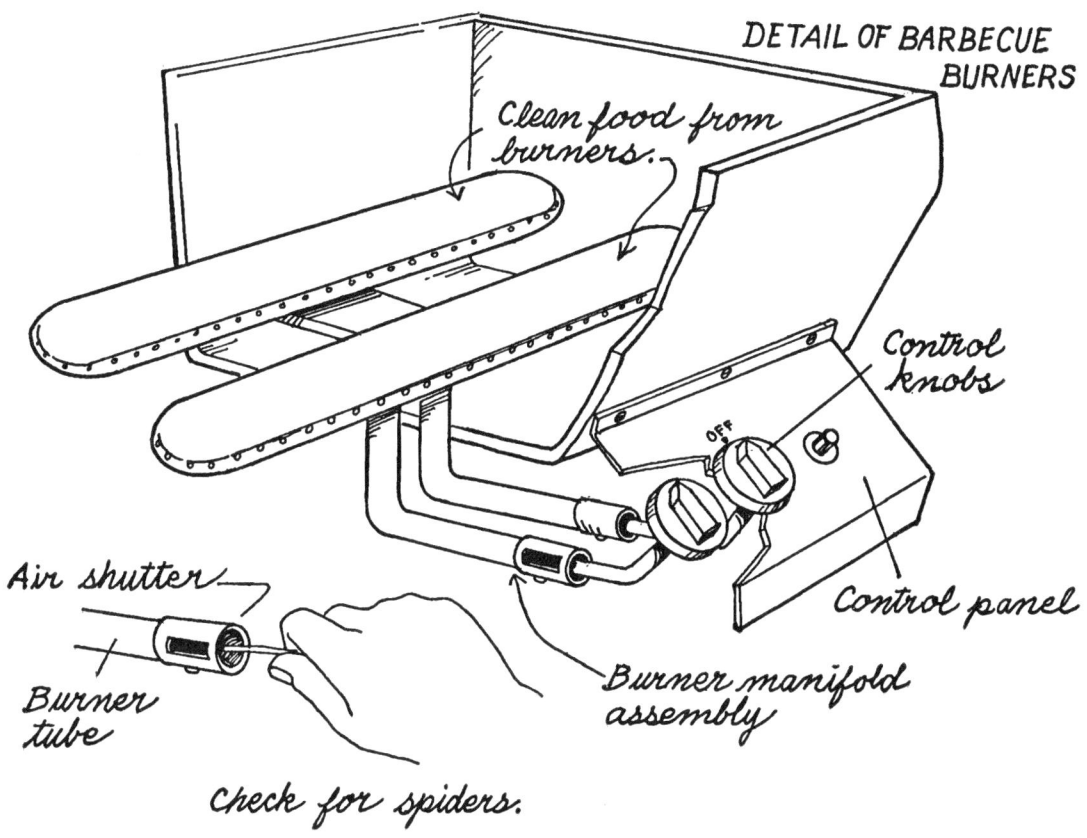

DETAIL OF BARBECUE BURNERS

Clean food from burners.

Control knobs

Control panel

Air shutter

Burner tube

Burner manifold assembly

Check for spiders.

BATHTUB, Caulk

Periodically check the bathtub caulk, which seals out water from penetrating behind the walls. To clean the caulk, use a toothbrush dipped in a paste made of borax and water or scouring foam. Carefully work out dirt and mildew from tight corners and crevices. If the caulk has pulled out of the joint or is missing, remove it completely with a putty knife and recaulk the bathtub.

The longest-lasting type of caulk is silicone. It comes in a full size $10^1/_2$-ounce tube, half tube, or squeeze tube. After making sure that the area is thoroughly dry and free of grit or dirt, apply the caulk to the joint between the bathtub and the wall around its perimeter.

11

BATHTUB, Fiberglass

After bathing or showering, wipe dry any water remaining in the tub with a rag. Clean away any dirt and soap scum that remain.

Even though fiberglass is a tough, durable surface, don't use a harsh abrasive cleaner or gritty scouring powder to clean it. Use a mild fiberglass cleaner or scrubbing foam to remove surface grit and grime. Thoroughly rinse the surface, paying special attention to corners and shelves or ledges where water can pool and accumulate. For a heavy buildup of dirt, use a sponge-covered wire mesh cleaning pad. To brighten a fiberglass bathtub, use a car wax or boat wax on the sides, but not on the tub floor, which might create a slippery surface.

BATHTUB, Porcelain finish on steel

To clean an old porcelain tub, use borax on a wet sponge or a bathtub scrubbing foam cleanser. If it's a tough stain, apply a paste of borax and water, then let it soak in for a while before scrubbing and rinsing. More than one application may be necessary. When the stain is removed, thoroughly rinse away the cleaning solution and run a dry rag around the tub to remove any water that remains.

Some new porcelain bathtubs can't withstand harsh scouring powders and should be cleaned with a milder scrubbing foam, as described for fiberglass tubs.

BATTERY, Alkaline

Alkaline batteries contain more energy than standard batteries and have a longer shelf life, typically 5–6 years. Alkaline batteries should be stored in a cool location but can be left in a flashlight or radio for long periods because they do not swell or leak as they age.

BATTERY, Rechargeable (nickel-cadmium or NiCad)

The useful life of a rechargeable battery can be maximized by keeping the battery fully charged. For this type of battery, only use a charger recommended by the manufacturer. Depending on the type of charger, it is possible to overcharge a battery by allowing it to remain in the charger indefinitely. So unless the manufacturer specifically states that you can leave the battery being charged without harm, remove the battery after an overnight charging.

You don't have to fully discharge a NiCad battery before recharging it. Newer NiCad batteries do not have a "memory" problem like some older ones that would lose some capacity if they were only partially discharged before being recharged.

If a battery seems to be accepting less of a charge, fully discharge it; then recharge it a few times to help restore it to full capacity.

Store in a cool location rechargeable batteries or any device containing rechargeable batteries with a full charge. Protect the batteries from freezing by storing them in a heated area. Do not throw any battery (rechargeable or otherwise) into a fireplace or incinerator because it may explode. Contact your local fire department about how to dispose of batteries properly.

BATTERY, Standard (carbon zinc)

All batteries have a limited shelf life and will eventually wear out, even if you don't use them. For example, a standard carbon zinc battery for a flashlight has an expected shelf life of 3–4 years. Before you purchase batteries, look at the expiration date.

Don't buy a large supply of batteries unless they are put to immediate use. Store unused batteries in a cool, dry location in their original containers.

Remove batteries from battery-operated devices that you don't use frequently (like a portable radio, flashlight, or tape recorder) and store the batteries separately, especially if they are run-down. Old batteries left in these household products for extended periods of time may develop leaks or swell and damage the device.

BEDSPRING

Once a year, remove the mattress from the bed so that its bedspring can be maintained. A vacuum's upholstery tool can be used to remove dust that has settled in the crevices of the binding. For a bed that is slept in on a daily basis, it's a good idea to reverse the bedspring head to foot so that the springs wear evenly. Lift the bedspring out of the bed frame and rotate it so the top is repositioned at the bottom.

To guard against mildew, spray disinfectant on the bedspring before reassembling the bed.

Today's multispeed bicycles are rather complex machines and require more upkeep than the older balloon-tire single-speed bikes. Whatever type of bicycle you have, a few minutes of maintenance *each season* will keep it running. A screwdriver, adjustable wrench, and a can of WD-40 go a long way toward keeping your bike in good working order.

Most bikes have metric nuts and bolts, so unless you have metric wrenches, use an adjustable wrench on all nuts. Remember, many of the fittings are aluminum, so don't overtighten the nuts and bolts. An all-purpose lubricant water displacer like WD-40 is easy to apply and effective for lubricating most parts of a bicycle.

The most important thing you can do to keep any bike running smoothly is to keep the tires inflated to the proper pressure. Underinflated tires make a bicycle harder to pedal and they can damage the wheel rims if you hit a curb or pothole. An underinflated tire is also more likely to go flat than a properly inflated one.

Inflate balloon tires to 30 to 60 pounds per square inch (PSI) and 70 to 125 PSI for 1$3/4$-inch or narrower tires. The maximum recommended pressure is imprinted on the tire; don't exceed it.

Hand brakes should be adjusted *yearly* or anytime you can squeeze the hand brake lever all the way to the handgrip. If you have a bike with coaster brakes they should be lubricated *annually* or when they squeak.

Inspect the cables leading from the hand brake levers to the wheel brakes, looking for broken strands of wire where they emerge from their housing at the brakes. Also squeeze the hand brake levers tightly and inspect the cables where they emerge from their housing at the levers. If you see a broken wire, take your bike to a repair shop because while replacing a brake cable is not too difficult, there are many varieties and sizes and the proper replacement is essential.

Also, inspect the brake pads and have the bike shop replace them if they are hard or cracked or less than $1/4$ inch thick.

If you want to make these repairs yourself, remove the cables by loosening the anchor bolts at the brakes and pull the cables out of their housing. Take them and the old brake pads to a bike store to get an exact replacement.

To adjust a bicycle's hand brakes, loosen the anchor bolt that holds the brake cable to the brake arm. It is usually located on the lower arm of sidepull brakes or in the center opposite the cable yoke on centerpull brakes. Have a helper squeeze the brake shoes firmly against the rim of the wheel while you pull the brake cable tight and tighten the locknut. Test its adjustment by spinning a wheel. It should turn without the brake pads hitting the rim.

If you have coaster (foot) brakes, add ten drops of lightweight machine oil to the oiling port located in the center of the rear wheel hub.

While you are spinning the wheels, wiggle them back and forth to check for movement in the bearing. The wheels should feel solid and not wiggle if you put side pressure on their rims. If they wiggle, take the bicycle to a repair shop to prevent serious damage to the wheel bearings.

If the bicycle chain is kept clean, your bike will be easier to ride and the chain will last a long time. Before you begin to clean it, place a layer of newspaper under the chain. Give it a liberal spraying of WD-40 to wash off most of the grime and dirt. Then wipe the chain dry and give it another squirting. Wait a few minutes and then wipe off as much of the WD-40 as possible.

There are gadgets sold at bike stores that clean and lubricate a bike chain in one step. You can clamp one device (which has cleaning brushes and a solvent/lubricant) over the chain and then pedal backward to pull the chain through the solvent. This method is less messy than wiping the chain clean with oil.

Keep the finish of a bike looking new with car wax polish. If you have a newer bike with a clear coat finish, be sure to use a nonabrasive polish.

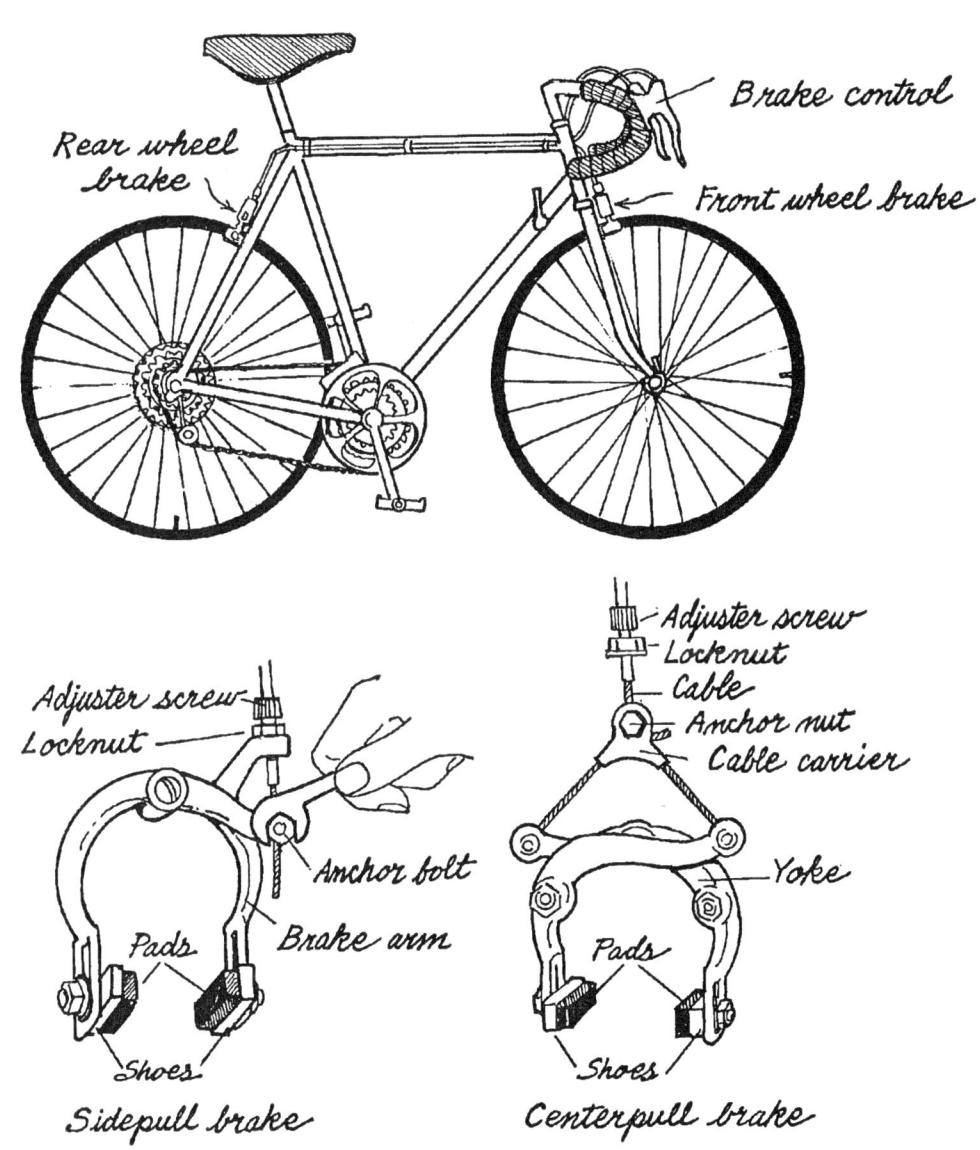

Rear wheel brake

Brake control

Front wheel brake

Adjuster screw
Locknut

Anchor bolt
Brake arm

Pads

Shoes

Sidepull brake

Adjuster screw
Locknut
Cable
Anchor nut
Cable carrier

Yoke

Pads

Shoes

Centerpull brake

BOILER

Few boilers in homes today actually boil water. Modern hydronic heating systems burn a fuel (gas, oil, electric) which heats water in the boiler to about 180–200 degrees. The hot water is then piped around your house to radiators or baseboard convectors.

The biggest enemy of a hydronic heating system is rust and corrosion. Small water leaks, especially those that drip directly on the boiler, will quickly turn it into a rust heap. The boiler itself has no moving parts but most systems have at least one or more circulator pumps that push the hot water through the system; oil-fired units also have a motor in the burner assembly.

At least once a year drain several gallons of water from the boiler to remove any buildup of dirt and corrosion within the unit. Connect a garden hose to the drain at the bottom of the boiler and lead it to a floor drain or into a bucket.

Correct any leaks. The safety pressure valve is prone to leak and it should be equipped with a drainpipe that carries water away from the boiler. Another source of potential leaks is any air bleeders installed in the system. These are devices located near the top of the boiler that hiss as air leaves the system, especially after the boiler has been drained and refilled. If they constantly leak, replace them.

The gaskets between the flanges of the circulator pump and boiler pipes harden and begin to crack over time. The joint is often a source of water leaks. Replacing these gaskets is not difficult since they are held in place by only two bolts.

Both the upper and lower gaskets should be replaced even if only one is leaking. First, turn off the power to the unit; then drain the boiler of water. You can connect a garden hose to a drain in the bottom of the boiler. Lead the hose to a floor drain. When the boiler is empty, remove the lower set of bolts first. Pry the pump and pipe flanges apart with a screwdriver and remove the gasket. Replace the gasket and tighten the bolts. Remove the upper gasket in the same way. If you can't pry the flanges apart, remove the upper set of bolts and pull the pump completely out. Then replace the gaskets and tighten the bolts.

If you have a steam system operating in your house, a professional experienced with this kind of boiler should service your unit. Maintaining a steam heating system is not a do-it-yourself project because of the very high temperatures and pressures associated with steam heat.

See also entries for "Furnace" (Gas, Oil) and "Radiator/Baseboard Convector."

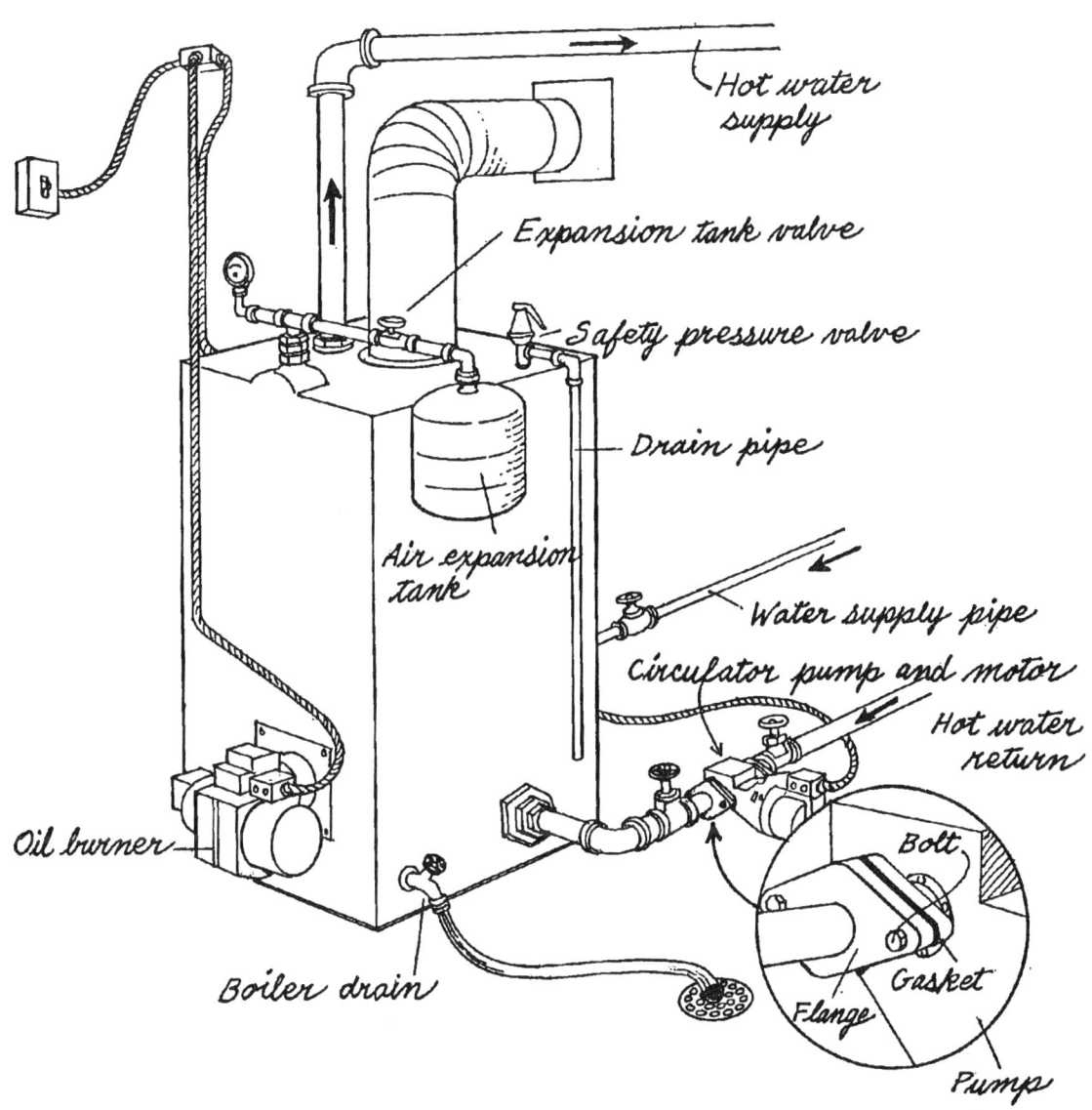

Hot water supply

Expansion tank valve

Safety pressure valve

Drain pipe

Air expansion tank

Water supply pipe

Circulator pump and motor

Hot water return

Oil burner

Boiler drain

Bolt

Gasket

Flange

Pump

BUTCHER BLOCK

The end grain of thick hardwood is a tough surface for chopping food in a kitchen. Butcher block is used as a countertop or a cutting board insert in the counter and is also a popular surface as a tabletop for contemporary furniture.

After every use surfaces used for food preparation should be cleaned with mild soap and water. *Periodically* wipe on mineral oil to protect the finish of a butcher block tabletop.

To rejuvenate a knife-scarred or stained surface, use a hook-type paint scraper and a sanding block (or finish sander). Begin by protecting the area surrounding the butcher block with masking tape. A stray swipe with the scraper or sander could damage the nearby countertop or wall coverings.

Using a sharp new blade in the scraper, hold it firmly while pressing down as you pull the scraper

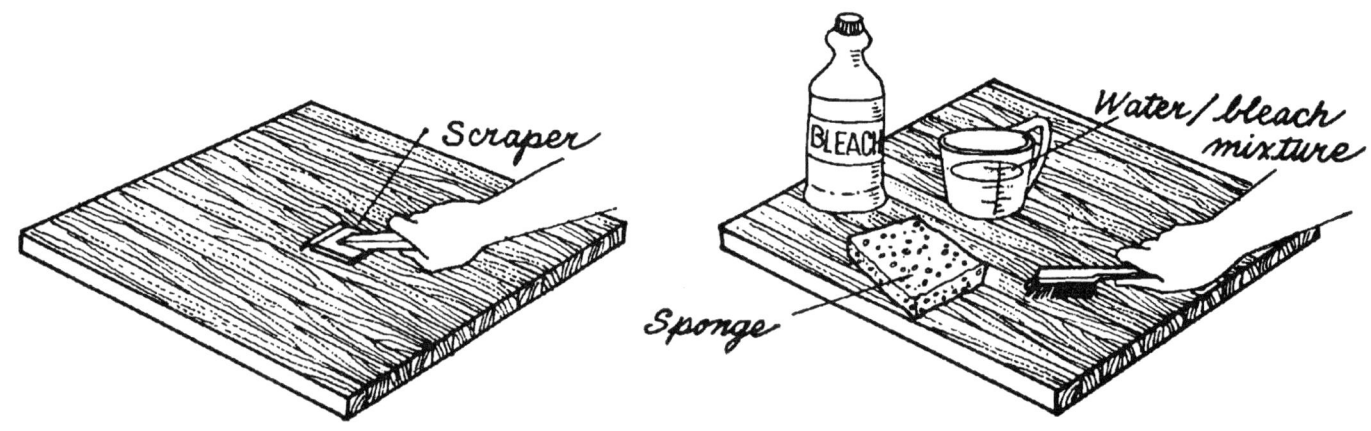

Scraper

BLEACH

Water/bleach mixture

Sponge

Sanding block with #120-grit sandpaper

18

toward you. You want to scrape off the old finish, any top-layer dirt, and high spots on the wood's surface. Using a scraper is faster than sanding the hardwood but it won't remove deep stain marks.

To remove dark stains or burn marks, scrape as much of the blemish away as possible, then follow with a thorough sanding, beginning with a heavy 80-grit sandpaper. Switch to a lighter 120-grit sandpaper to finish sanding the surface. Carefully sand the butcher block that adjoins other counter surfaces.

To brighten the surface and to help hide dark spots and stains, apply a mixture of half household bleach and half water with a sponge or soft rag. Let the surface dry. For stained areas or burn marks, apply bleach full strength. To neutralize the bleach, wipe the surface with a rag soaked in household white vinegar. Then wash the area with a mild soap and water and let it dry thoroughly. Since the water solution raises the grain of the wood, give the surface a light sanding with 120-grit sandpaper.

Finish treating the butcher block with mineral oil wherever food has come in regular contact with the wood. (The oil is nontoxic and free of harmful ingredients.) Let the bottle of mineral oil set in a pan of hot water for 15 minutes—to thin the oil in order to help it penetrate deeply into the surface. Apply the mineral oil with a soft rag and let it soak in. Wipe up the excess oil with paper towels. If you want a slight sheen, buff the butcher block with a soft rag.

To rejuvenate a tabletop or counter with a butcher block surface, sand it lightly with 100-grit sandpaper or a sanding block. Apply tung oil with a soft rag and when it's dry, buff it to a shine. For even more shine, apply several coats of tung oil.

CAMERA, 35mm

If you treat a good camera and its lenses with respect, they will reward you with years of faithful service. Store a camera that won't be used for several months with the meter and flash batteries removed, because an old battery can leak, causing damage to the interior of the camera.

Dirt is the greatest enemy of any camera. Inside the camera, dirt causes spots in pictures and eventually works its way deep inside and gums up the mechanical parts. On a camera lens, dirt degrades the image quality.

Keep the camera exterior (not including the lens) clean with a dry, soft rag. When you clean the exterior, leave the lens on the camera body to prevent any dirt from getting inside. Purchase a blower brush (a small camel hair brush attached to a rubber bulb) at your local photography store. This is handy for cleaning difficult-to-reach crevices around the camera controls. Dust and dirt also collect in the viewing window, so dust it off with the brush and clean the glass surface with a soft rag.

When the exterior is clean, open the camera and clean its interior. Inspect it for film chips left in the winding mechanism. Carefully clean the film guides and pressure plate on the back of the camera. Don't attempt to clean the shutter; just blow off any dust or dirt with a blower brush. Close the back of the camera.

Remove the lens and use the blower brush to remove dirt from the reflex mirror. Do not touch

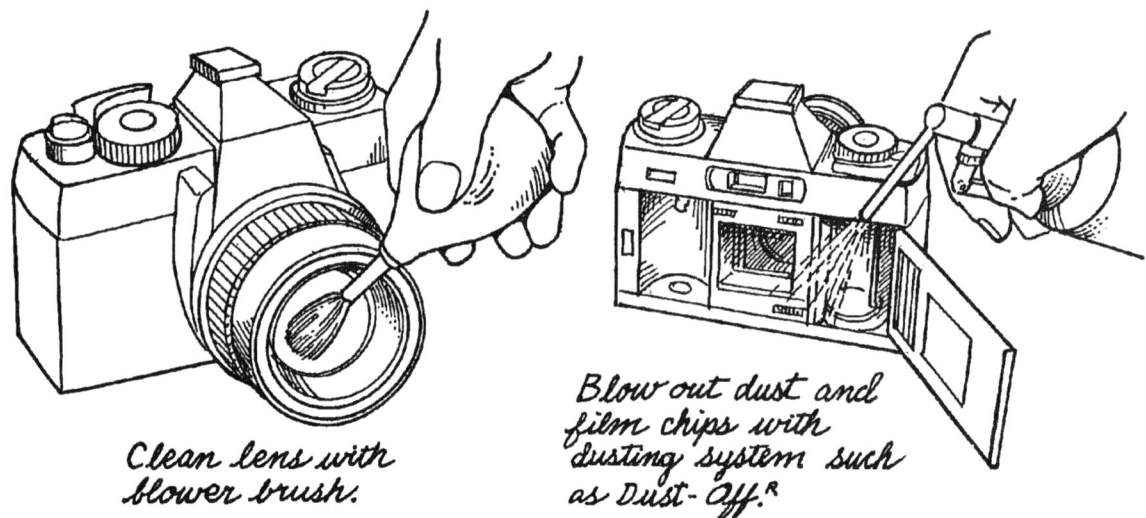

Clean lens with
blower brush.

Blow out dust and
film chips with
dusting system such
as Dust-Off.®

the mirror with your fingers. Unlike a standard mirror, it has a silver mirror surface applied to the top surface of the glass and your fingerprints can damage this coating.

The secret to keeping your camera lens in top shape is to protect its coated glass surface with an inexpensive UV or daylight filter. This filter screws into the front of the lens and prevents dust from settling on the glass. When you clean the lens, you actually clean this filter and not the lens element.

Before you clean any glass surface, blow as much dirt off as possible with the blower brush. Use a piece of lint-free lens tissue to clean any glass surface. If you must dampen the lens surface, breathe on the glass so that a light haze forms on its surface. Avoid using lens cleaning fluid if possible. If you do, apply it to the lens tissue to dampen it, and not directly to the lens element.

CAN OPENER, Electric

Observe how your can opener works and you'll notice that a small cutter wheel is forced into the edge of the can lid when you push the operating lever down. The can is then turned by the motor-driven gear which grips the top flange of the can. If the teeth on the gear are worn or the cutter wheel does not turn freely, the can opener will work unreliably. The cutter wheel and drive gear are hardworking parts and after repeated use food dries and cakes around them, eventually causing the bearings to squeak and then fail.

Unplug the can opener from the electrical outlet before working on it. Clean the cutter wheel with a toothbrush or other small stiff brush to remove

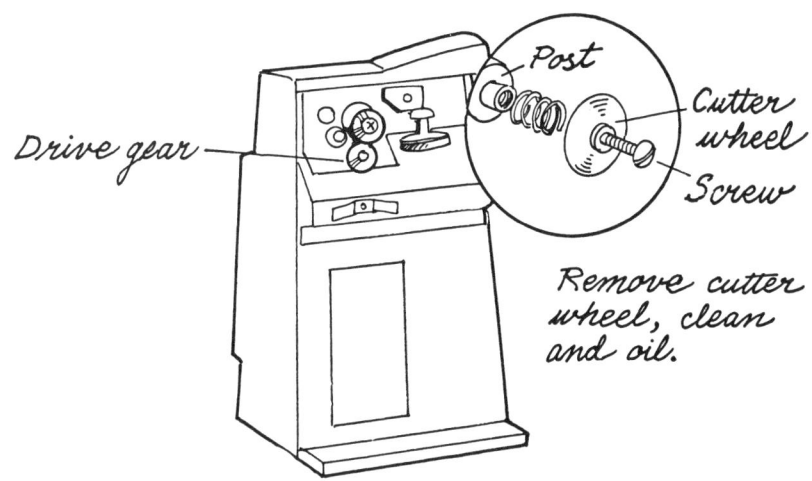

Drive gear

Post

Cutter wheel

Screw

Remove cutter wheel, clean and oil.

food and dirt. Check that the wheel turns freely. If it doesn't, put on a pair of work gloves to protect your hands from the sharp wheel and give it a couple of turns. Turn the wheel back and forth to loosen the bearings. Then apply a couple of drops of a light household oil. Wipe any excess oil off the cutter wheel with a paper towel.

Clean and lubricate the drive gear in the same way. Remove food or small metal particles from the gear teeth so that the drive gear can get a good grip on the can.

CARPETING / RUGS

Your trusty vacuum cleaner is the most effective method to easily remove dirt, crumbs, and dust from carpet and rug fibers. There is usually a buildup of dirt where foot traffic is the heaviest, near frequently used pieces of furniture (e.g., in front of the family room sofa or under the dining table). In rooms with wall-to-wall carpeting there is often a line of dust around the perimeter of the room and often near the outlet for heating and cooling ducts.

Vacuum whenever and wherever it's necessary in order to maintain carpet fibers. *At least four times a year* move furniture in order to vacuum thoroughly all areas of wall-to-wall carpeting.

To prevent wall-to-wall carpeting from being worn and matted down in certain areas, rearrange the furniture in a room *once a year*. Begin this practice with new carpeting and it will "age" evenly. With area rugs this can be done by rotating them within a room or changing them from one room to another.

When an accident happens, wipe up the stain as

soon as possible with paper towels. Follow the directions on spot removers and carpet cleaning agents for best results in removing the stain.

Once a year remove area rugs for airing outdoors. Before you take a rug outside, vacuum it, then roll it up for easier carrying. If possible, shake out the rug and then drape it over two parallel clotheslines or spread it on a deck or patio. Don't leave it in harsh direct sun for an extended period of time, which can result in bleached-out colors. If there are pets in the house do this more frequently and use a carpet deodorizer.

For a thorough rug cleaning you can hire a carpet cleaning service or do it yourself with a rental carpet cleaning machine. These are available for rent at most hardware stores and home centers. Follow the directions and avoid soaking the carpet with water.

CHIMNEY, Brick, Cinder block, Steel

Once a year inspect the interior lining of your house's chimney for a buildup of creosote (which looks like heavy black tar) or soot. To do this, first open the damper in the fireplace and look up the chimney. If it looks shiny inside or if you can't see all the way up the chimney, use a sturdy ladder to go on the roof (be very careful!) and look down the chimney flue.

A shiny coating on the inside of the flue is a sure sign of a creosote buildup, which can be dangerous. If you have a $1/8$-inch or more coating of creosote on the chimney liner, call a chimney sweep to do the job before you use the fireplace again.

To remove a thin lining of soot or creosote, purchase a chimney brush, a long-handled wire brush that comes in various diameters to fit different-sized flues. It is sold by retailers who specialize in wood-burning stoves and fireplaces.

Before doing any work on the interior walls of the chimney, be sure that you take steps to protect the interior of the house. For a fireplace, use duct tape and heavy plastic garbage bags to enclose and tightly seal the open hearth area so that debris doesn't enter. Remove furnishings around the fireplace and lay dropcloths on the floor surrounding the hearth. For a wood-burning stove, remove the chimney connector pipe and cover the flue opening with tape and plastic.

Up on the roof, work the brush back and forth on the side walls of the chimney, causing the soot and debris to fall into the pipe. Carefully collect and remove the debris from inside the house.

Also inspect the chimney and roof area for signs of wear. Loose bricks should be repointed and flashing (sheets of metal or other material used for weatherproofing) should be replaced if it is worn or damaged. Relocate any empty birds' nests to a safer location.

CLOSET DOOR, Folding

A folding closet door relies on its hinges for support and a track installed on the top of the jamb for guidance. For the door to operate smoothly, the hinges must be tight and the top track and guide have to be clean.

A folding door is maintenance-free as long as all the hinge screws remain tight and the door doesn't sag. If you notice any binding of the guide mechanism during opening or closing, check that the hinge screws are tight. If loose screws are neglected, they can gradually loosen as they are worked in and out of their holes when the door is opened and closed. Eventually screw holes in the wood enlarge and the screws lose their grip on the door. This causes the door to sag and bind.

Clean the top track and lightly lubricate it with a spray silicone. Spray some lubricant on the guide wheel or pin so that it operates smoothly in the track.

A four-panel door has a set of stops or guides installed on the floor where the doors meet. Check to see that they're not bent or loose. Replacement guides, which are sold in home centers and hardware stores, can be easily installed.

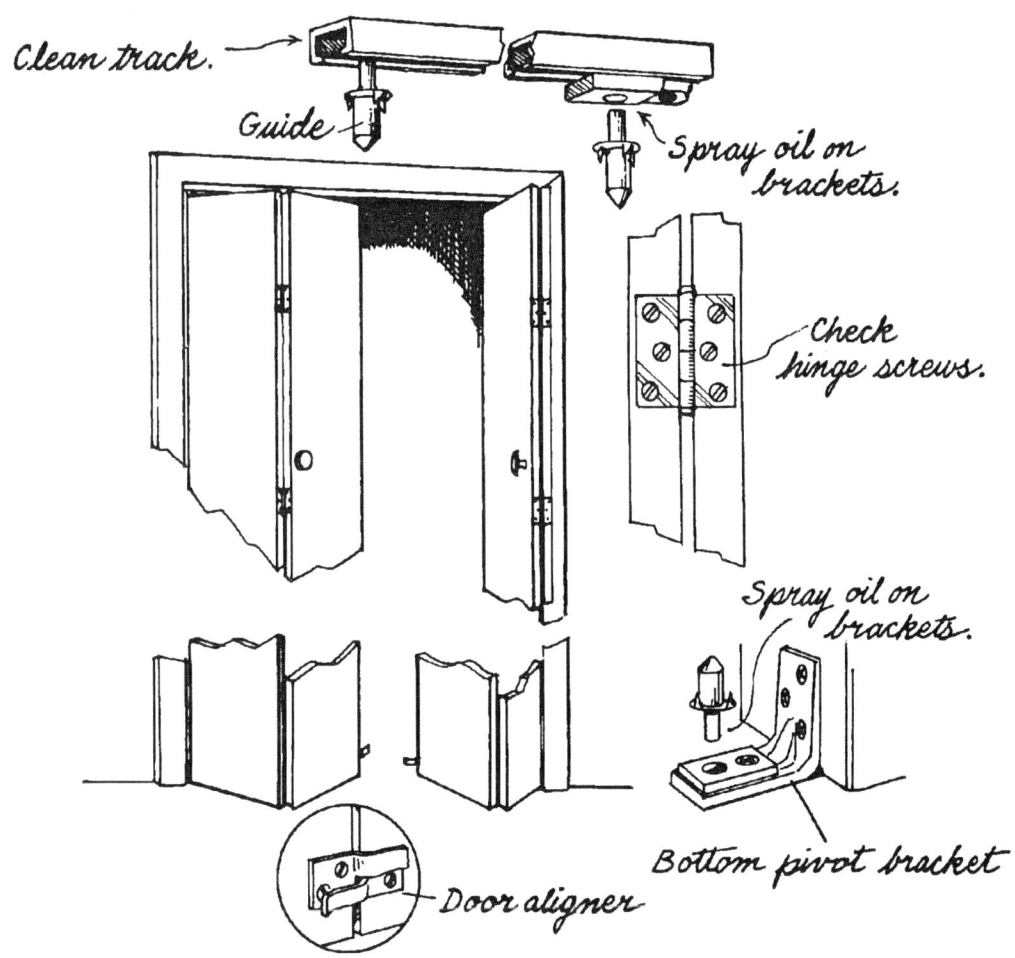

Clean track.

Guide

Spray oil on brackets.

Check hinge screws.

Spray oil on brackets.

Bottom pivot bracket

Door aligner

CLOSET DOOR, Sliding

Sliding doors roll on an overhead track secured to the top of the door jamb. Eventually dust and dirt can settle in the track and gum up the roller wheels. Gummed-up rollers do not turn easily and can create a lot of friction between the rollers and the track. As this situation gets worse, more and more effort is needed to open and close the door, and eventually you have to push so hard that the track or rollers can become bent or permanently damaged.

Periodic cleaning of this track and lubrication of the rollers will keep the mechanism running smoothly. Every time you vacuum the floor, use the vacuum's crevice tool to clean out the closet door's track. When necessary, give the rollers and track a light spraying of silicone; don't overdo it because the lubricant can attract dirt.

If you notice a problem as you open or close the door, do some investigating. The door may have jumped off its track and needs to be repositioned, or the rollers may need a little lubrication.

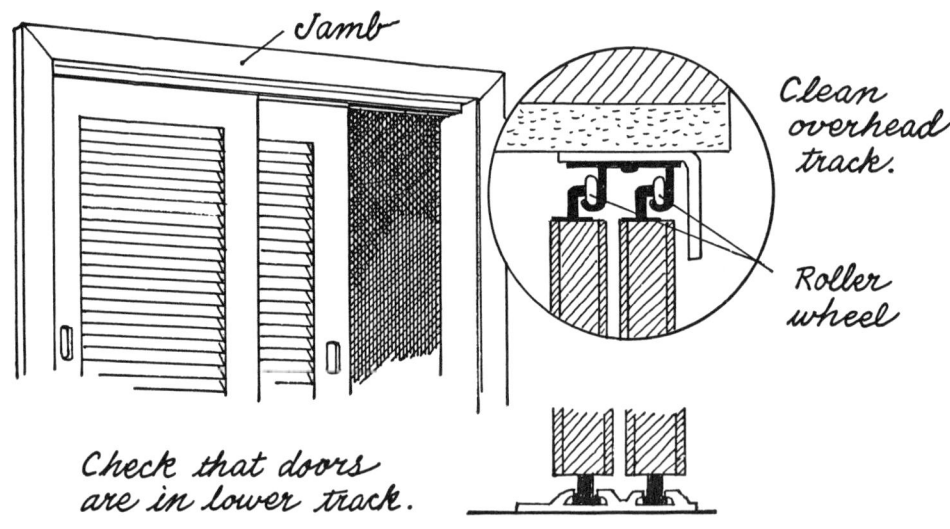

Jamb

Clean overhead track.

Roller wheel

Check that doors are in lower track.

CLOTHES DRYER, Electric

An electric clothes dryer circulates a lot of air through it. Any restriction in the flow of this air and your dryer cannot operate efficiently. *After every use* of the dryer, remove lint from the lint filter. *Periodically* check the dryer vent, at the back of the dryer, for a buildup of lint and dust, and use the crevice tool of your vacuum to remove this accumulation. *Once a year* remove the service panel to vacuum any lint that has accumulated around the heater housing and motor. The lint and dust are flammable and can cause a fire hazard if they build up.

Inspect the duct that carries the hot air away from the dryer to see that it's straight, not kinked. If there are signs of wear or small holes, patch the damaged area with gray duct tape.

Clean the dryer with a mild soap when necessary and wipe off any spilled cleaning products as soon as possible.

After drying heavy rugs or fabrics, a dryer sometimes wiggles or shimmies out of position so it is no longer level. If that happens, check to see if it is sitting firmly on the floor by trying to rock it back and forth. If it wobbles, it needs adjustment.

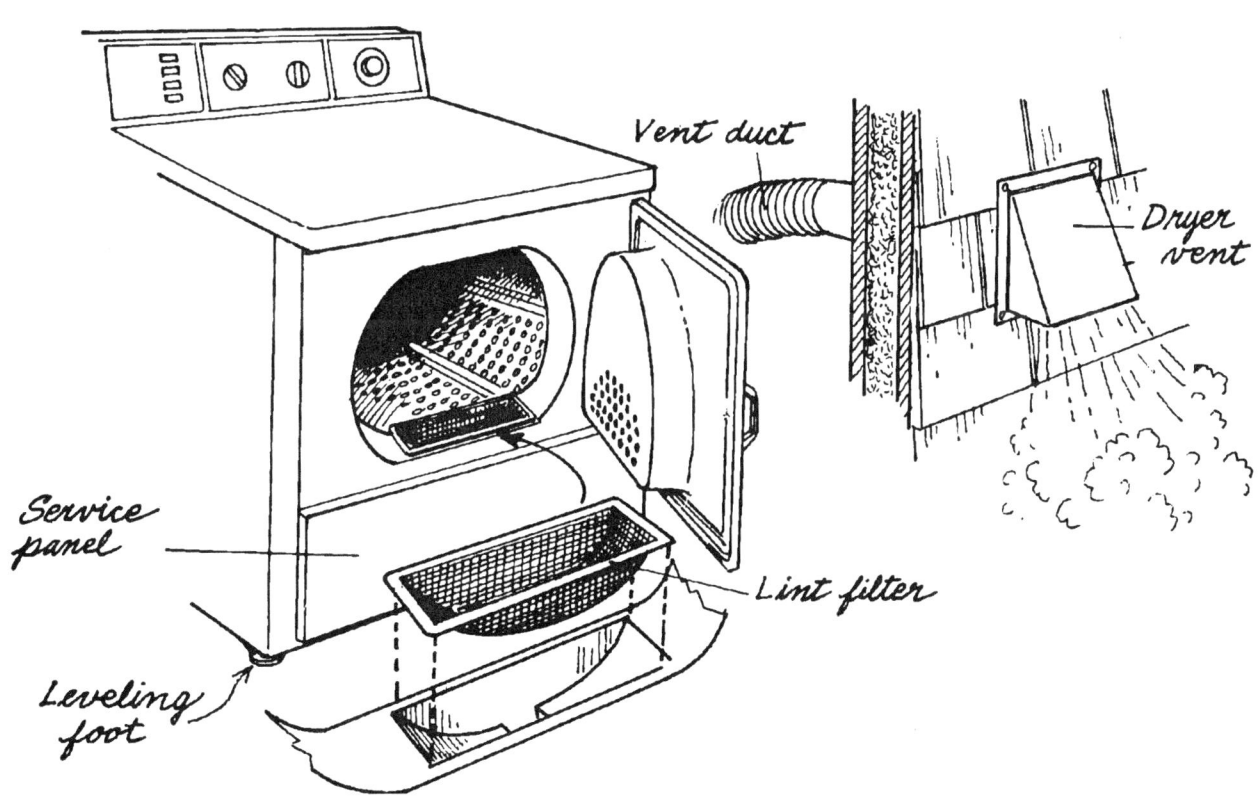

Vent duct

Dryer vent

Service panel

Lint filter

Leveling foot

To level the dryer, turn the dryer control to "Off" and unplug the unit from the electrical outlet. Place a carpenter's level on top of the dryer. Then get down on your hands and knees with an adjustable wrench and flashlight to look for the four leveling feet that are located at the corners of the machine. The sheet metal housing or the leveling feet may have sharp edges, so be careful; don't poke your hand underneath the dryer without using the flashlight to see what you're doing.

Each leveling foot has a jamb nut that holds the foot to the bottom of the dryer. Use the adjustable wrench to position the front feet first. Loosen the jamb nut and screw the leveling foot in or out, depending on whether the dryer needs to be lowered or raised to center the bubble on the carpenter's level. Sometimes all four feet require adjusting, often it's just one of them. When the machine rests solidly on all four feet and is level (right to left and front to back), tighten the locking screws on each foot. Then plug the dryer back in and it's ready to be used.

CLOTHES DRYER, Gas

Gas dryer maintenance is basically the same as for an electric dryer. In addition to keeping the lint filter clean, check for an accumulation of lint around the gas burner assembly. Lint is flammable and, if allowed to accumulate inside the dryer for long periods, it can pose a fire threat.

CLOTHES IRON, Steam

When water turns to steam inside a steam iron, all the impurities contained in the water are left behind. These deposits can build up inside the iron over time and clog the steam ports and water chamber. Your steam iron will last longer if mineral-free water is used.

Don't store the iron for long periods of time with a full water reservoir. Unplug the iron and let it cool, and empty the water by holding the iron over a sink. To release the water, turn the iron upside down with the sole plate facing upward and the tip of the iron pointed down. (This procedure prevents water from running into the steam chamber and causing the iron to spit water the next time you use it.)

CLOTHES WASHER

Rust is probably the biggest enemy your clothes washer has to face. ***After every use*** leave the lid open so that moisture inside can evaporate. Check to see that the hot and cold water hoses are not kinked and that the hose filters are not clogged with lint.

The washer must be level for it to work properly. If the washer tilts, it will cause excessive wear to the bearings that hold the tub in place. Also, a unit that is not level will not spin a full load without tripping the out-of-balance safety switch on the washer. *(See page 26, for how to level a clothes dryer.)*

Before you perform any maintenance on your clothes washer, it must be unplugged. Turn the water off at the hot and cold water outlets. Loosen the water intake hoses at the back of the machine with a channel-lock pliers and remove them from the hot and cold water outlets.

Pull out the small round washers containing the fine screen hose filters. If they won't come out, pry them loose with a screwdriver. If they show signs of wear or are badly corroded, take them to a hardware store to buy replacement screens. If the screens are covered with mineral deposits, wash them and replace them in the hose. Then reattach the hose to the hot and cold faucets, making

Filter

Hot and cold water outlets

Water intake hoses

Pantyhose filter

sure that you connect the hot and cold hoses to the corresponding faucet.

If your clothes washer empties into a wash sink, keep lint from clogging the drain by making a lint strainer from a piece of old pantyhose. Cut the leg off about 12 inches up from the toe and secure it to the end of the discharge hose with a 1½-inch-diameter hose clamp.

To break down soap scum buildup in the washing machine and its hoses, run the machine through a full cycle with warm water and a cup of white vinegar. Repeat the cycle with another wash using a cup of household bleach.

COFFEE MAKER, Automatic drip

To make better tasting and faster brewing coffee, flush out the coffee maker with white household vinegar. The vinegar removes hard water mineral buildup on the heating element. If you use the unit every day, flush it out **every three months.** For less frequent use, flush it out **every four to five months.**

Fill the carafe to the full capacity mark with a half water and half vinegar mixture. Pour the mixture into the unit as if you were making coffee and then turn the machine on. When the water-vinegar mixture has completed the brewing cycle, repeat with a flush cycle of clear water. When the cycle is completed, your coffee maker is ready to use.

Clean the outside of the appliance with a rag dampened in soapy water; don't immerse it in water. Wash a glass carafe with mild soap and water, and rinse thoroughly. Wipe or air dry.

For a thermal carafe, rinse it with soap and water, but don't immerse it. Let it air dry. Don't use abrasive cleaners or scouring pads on any plastic or glass parts and don't put the unit in a dishwasher.

To remove coffee stains, fill the carafe with hot water and a denture-cleansing tablet and let it stand for 10 minutes. Then rinse the carafe with water.

COMPACT DISC PLAYER

Unless you have considerable experience tinkering with electronic devices there isn't much that the average user can do to service a CD player. As with most home electronic gadgets, dust and dirt are their worst enemies, so a routine cleaning is the best preventive maintenance you can perform.

When not in use, keep the compact disc loading drawer closed so that airborne dust doesn't settle on the tray and get carried inside when the drawer is closed. Clean the drawer with a damp lint-free cloth. Do not use strong household cleaners, which can be harmful to the molded plastic part of the drawer.

To keep compact discs clean, purchase a

cleaning kit (found at home electronics stores) and use it sparingly. Keep your compact discs clean, but don't get carried away. Most manufacturers recommend that you remove fingerprints and smudges, but a little dust will not affect the CDs' performance.

You can clean a compact disc with a soft lint-free rag dampened in disc cleaning fluid or ethyl alcohol. Holding its edge, wipe the disc with strokes radiating outward from its center in order to remove fingerprints or dirt. Never use a household cleaner or solvent; clean your discs only with products recommended by the manufacturer.

Unplug the CD player before cleaning it. Clean the cable contacts at the back of the player and the amplifier or tuner *at least once a year.* Pull the phono plugs at the ends of the cables out of their sockets and clean the socket and plug. If the phono plugs or their mating terminal on the CD player or amplifier appear dirty, clean them with a cotton swab dipped in ethyl alcohol. When they're dry, reinsert them into the proper terminals. Then twist

them back and forth to seat them securely and assure good contact.

Avoid mishandling the CD player and protect it from temperature extremes and excessive humidity and moisture.

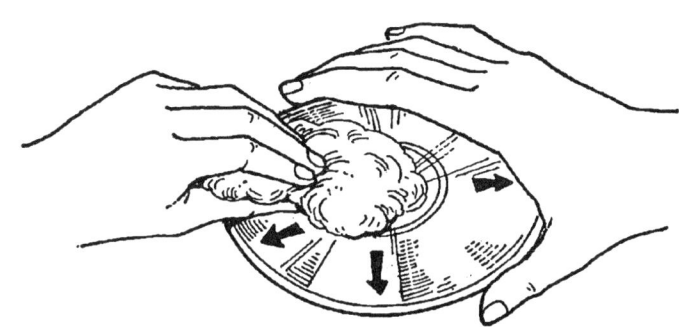

Clean compact disc with a soft rag, starting in the center and stroking outward.

COMPUTER

To keep a computer in good working condition, place it in a "healthy" environment with plenty of air circulation around it. When a computer is not in use, protect its keyboard, monitor screen, and printer with an anti-static dust cover.

Use the crevice tool of a vacuum to remove dust and dirt that has settled inside the keyboard. A hand-held computer vacuum, sold in computer stores and through computer mail-order sources, is specially designed for this purpose. Clean the

computer's keys and case with a soft damp cloth. There are cleaning solutions specifically made for cleaning the keyboard and other plastic parts but a dampened rag dipped in water works fine, too. Do not use harsh household cleaners or any solvent-based cleaner on the plastic parts. Clean the screen with a soft rag dampened with window cleaner; don't spray it on. Do not use strong household cleaners or those with abrasive elements. You will find a whole array of cleaning aids at most large computer stores. They carry presaturated cleaning pads and static-free cloths and cleaning fluids especially formulated for computers.

Most manufacturers recommend cleaning the floppy disk drive *periodically.* Purchase a cleaning kit for either a 5¼-inch disk or 3½-inch disk, or one for each if you have two different-sized floppy disk drives in your system. Follow the instructions provided in the disk cleaning kit. Unless your system has no hard disk drive and has only floppy disks, cleaning *once or twice a year* is sufficient.

Don't eat or drink around the computer. If you do and accidentally spill some liquid on the keyboard, turn the computer off immediately. Unplug the keyboard from the computer and turn it upside down so that the liquid can drain. Set the keyboard aside to dry overnight before you attempt to use it again.

COMPUTER PRINTER

While most computer printers are designed to require little routine maintenance, there are a few things you can do to assure that they stay reliable. Check your owner's manual for particular maintenance routines. Turn the computer and the printer off before you do any cleaning or maintenance.

When your printer is not being used, protect it from dust and dirt by covering it. If you do this religiously, most of the other tasks will be easy.

At least once a month, more often if your printer is in a dusty or smoke-filled area, use a computer vacuum or crevice tool to vacuum the interior in order to remove paper dust and other debris. Be careful not to damage the flex ribbon cable and the carriage drive belt. Then wipe the case with a damp soft rag. Don't use harsh household cleaners or abrasive cleaners.

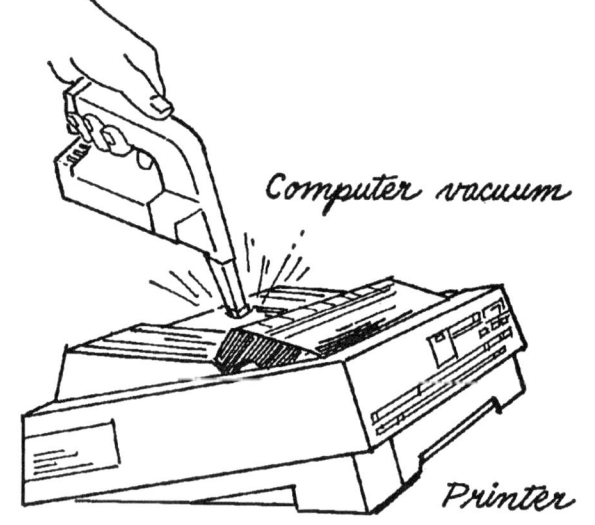

Computer vacuum

Printer

DECK, Cedar, Redwood, and Pressure-treated lumber

Exposure to the sun and water damage are the two biggest threats that a deck faces. The best way to keep decking in good shape is to remove wet leaves and debris that can stain the wood and promote the growth of rot and mildew. **During the winter,** remove large chunks of frozen snow and ice that can loosen the decking as it expands and contracts during its thaw-freeze cycles.

Periodically check the deck for popped nail heads that protrude above the surface. Hammer these nails flush in order to secure the decking and to prevent injury to bare feet. Also, remove any splinters and sand any area of rough wood with a medium-weight sandpaper.

Once a season remove all the furniture, plants, etc., and sweep the deck so that it's free of leaves and debris. Then scrub the deck with a mild soap and water mixture. Allow it to dry completely. Protect the clean decking from the sun's ultraviolet rays by applying a water repellent that contains a UV (ultraviolet) inhibitor.

The easiest method to apply the sealer is with a

Soap and water

Stiff brush

paint roller. Prevent back strain by purchasing an inexpensive extension pole that screws into the handle of the roller handle. Pour the water repellent into the roller pan and then dip the roller into the pan. Apply water repellent to the decking near the house first, and gradually work further away so you don't splash it. To get the repellent into tight areas like corners and between railing spindles, use a heavy bristle paintbrush.

Carefully apply the repellent to the end grain of the decking and the exposed end grain of deck beams and posts. Wood absorbs water more easily at its ends, so apply the sealer generously to this area. Allow it to soak in, then apply a second or third coat until the sealer stays wet-looking, a sign that the wood won't absorb any more sealer.

If the deck has been neglected and shows signs of fungus and mildew, scrub it before you apply the sealer. A bristle broom brush and a biodegradable soap and water is the most sensitive approach. For tough stains, use a deck cleaner, which contains chemicals that remove dirt and mildew along with some of the gray surface fibers. Before buying a deck cleaner, look at the label to see if the ingredients can cause harm to gardens or lawns.

To restore the natural wood color of a deck, use a deck restorer or brightener, which bleaches out stains and dirt. These products contain potent, caustic ingredients, so read the labels carefully. Protect yourself with rubber gloves and eye protection. Also protect the surrounding shrubbery and nearby plants with plastic tarpaulins. Be sure to keep children and pets clear of the area while you are using these products.

Deck brighteners can be applied with a garden-type sprayer, but don't use one that has been used to apply garden insect or weed killers. You can purchase an inexpensive sprayer designed for this job. Follow the manufacturer's directions carefully. Some deck brighteners and restorers must be allowed to sink into the dirty wood for a while before they are rinsed off. Others require chemical neutralizing after use.

When your deck is clean and bright, treat it with a finish coat of water repellent or stain to keep it looking good. If you keep the wood sealed, you will not have to use harsh chemical cleaners.

DEHUMIDIFIER

A dehumidifier is actually a small air conditioner with both the condensing and evaporator coils inside its cabinet. The compressor cools the evaporator coil just like an air conditioner. The fan draws damp air over the coil, cooling the air and forcing the excess moisture to condense on it. The air then passes over the warm condensing coil and is reheated to nearly room temperature.

Like an air conditioner, a dehumidifier processes a lot of air through its coils and requires regular cleaning. Unlike a humidifier, a dehumidifier condenses mineral-free water out of the air and therefore doesn't build up large mineral deposits.

Monthly summer maintenance will keep a unit running right. Dirt is a good insulator so any buildup on the coils will make them less effective. A dirty motor will run hotter than necessary and shorten its life, so use the crevice attachment of your vacuum to remove dust and dirt from inside the case and around the coils and motor. Unplug the dehumidifier and allow the coils to dry.

Consult the owner's manual for directions on how to remove the dehumidifier's cover. Most of them lift or slide off, but some are held in place by a couple of sheet metal screws. Remove the cover and vacuum any dirt from both coils. Note that the dirt collects on the side of the coils that faces the air flow. When the coils are clean, carefully straighten any of the small bent fins. Separate any of the fins that are pushed together so that air can pass between each fin.

Many dehumidifiers have an overflow switch which shuts the unit off when the collection bucket is full. Check that this switch is free of dirt and that the float lever moves freely.

Once a season, lubricate the motor shaft with a couple of drops of 20-weight machine oil placed on the fan shaft where it enters the motor. Check your owner's manual because many of the newer units have motors with permanently oiled bearings. In any case, don't over-oil because the excess will attract dirt and do more harm to the motor than help it. The compressor motor doesn't require any maintenance since it is a sealed unit.

If there is a drain hose connected to the unit, check to see that the drain hole in the water collection bucket is not clogged. ***In the off season,*** remove the hose and store it in a loose coil so that it's not bent or twisted.

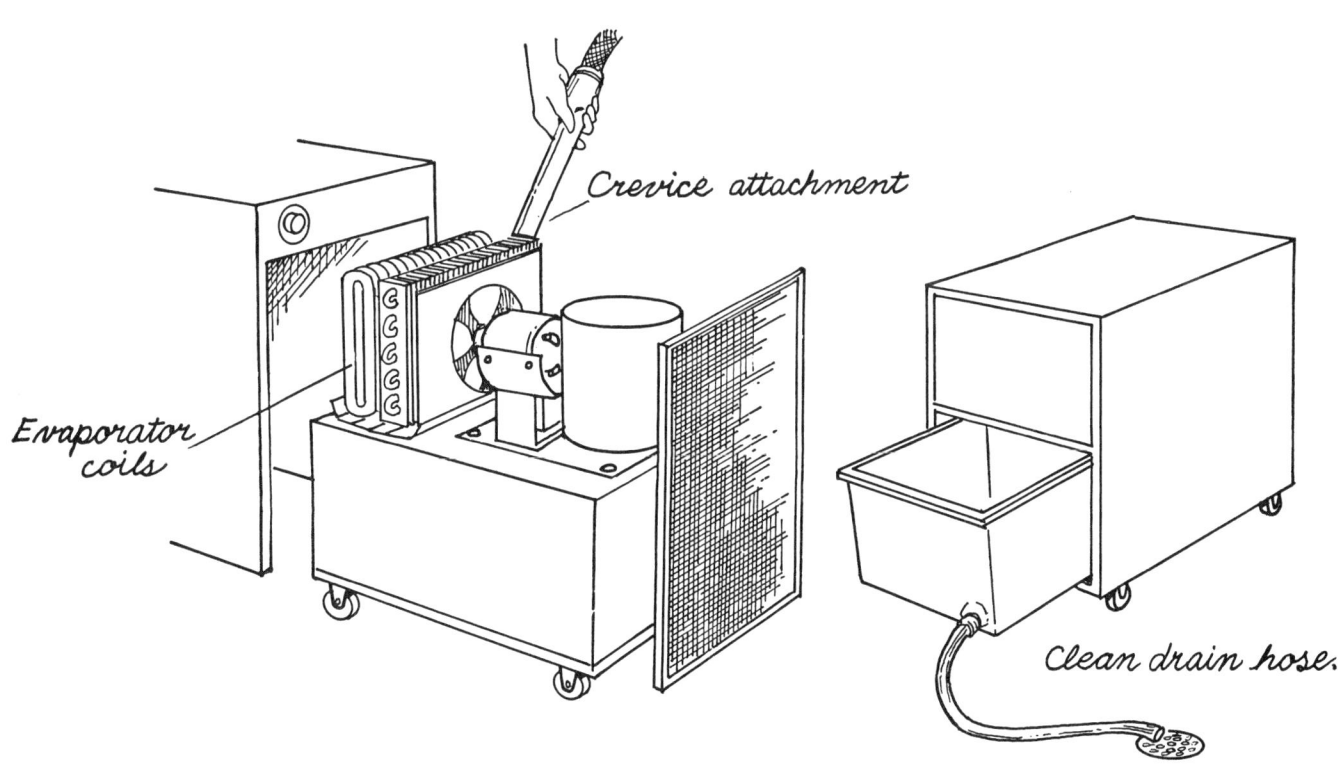

Crevice attachment

Evaporator coils

Clean drain hose.

The more water that your dishwasher can throw at your dirty dishes, the cleaner they will be. To keep a dishwasher working at top efficiency, **periodically** check to see that the pump screen and spray arm holes are free of small food particles and other deposits.

The pump screen is usually located in the well at the base of the unit. Some units don't have a screen, so if you don't see an obvious opening in the bottom of the dishwasher with a screen on it, you may have one of these models.

Remove any large food particles from the pump screen with your fingers, then scrub the screen filter clean with a stiff toothbrush or other small brush.

The holes in the rotating spray arm in the center of the dishwasher can also get clogged. Remove the spray arm. The lower arms will most likely lift off of their brackets but they may be held in place with a nut. The overhead arms will probably snap in place or be secured with a nut. These arms are easily removable, but check your owner's manual in any case.

Use a straightened paper clip or piece of thin wire to unclog any holes that you cannot see through in the spray arms. Poke the wire through the hole and wiggle it back and forth to dislodge the dirt or food particles. When all the holes are open, turn the arm so that the large center opening that fits on the shaft faces down. Then shake the hollow arm so all the small particles fall out of the opening. If you don't get most of these loose particles out of the arm, they will reclog it as soon as you run the dishwasher.

Periodically clean the interior sides and door by washing them down with a paste of baking soda

Clean pump screen.

Clean spray arm water outlet.

and water. Use a sponge to wipe off stains (if they're stubborn, let the paste set for a while) and remove tough areas with a scrubbing pad.

Keep the soap dispenser compartment clean and check that the door closes easily. If the door to this compartment sticks shut, the soap is not released and it will cake up in the compartment. Usually all that is needed to get the door working again is to clean the excess soap from the compartment. Remove the excess soap, and clean the compartment and the area around the door.

Keep the door panel—and/or all four sides of the unit if it's a portable dishwasher—clean by washing it with a mild soap and water solution. For spotted areas, which are especially noticeable on black glass fronts, use a damp sponge dipped in borax. Rinse with water and dry with a soft rag.

Daily use of your dishwasher keeps water in the bottom of the tub, which lubricates the rubber seals in the unit and pump. If you're going to be away for several months, pour an ounce of cooking oil into the puddle of standing water in order to keep it from evaporating. This helps prevent the rubber parts from drying out and shrinking while the machine isn't in use.

In addition to splashing water around, a dishwasher requires hot water to work efficiently. Check the water temperature at the nearest faucet to the dishwasher. Run the water into a glass and place a candy or meat thermometer in the glass. Allow the water to run until the temperature doesn't rise. If it's not at least 140 degrees, turn the temperature up on your water heater. Don't set it any higher or you will be wasting energy.

DOOR CLOSER

A pneumatically operated door closer is very reliable and doesn't require much attention, but a little tender loving care **once a year,** following the suggestions given here, will extend its life almost indefinitely.

Open the door so that the closer is completely extended. The rod that extends out of the closer body (piston assembly) should be clean and shiny. If it isn't, use an oily rag to clean this rod because any accumulation of dirt or rust will cause the seal in

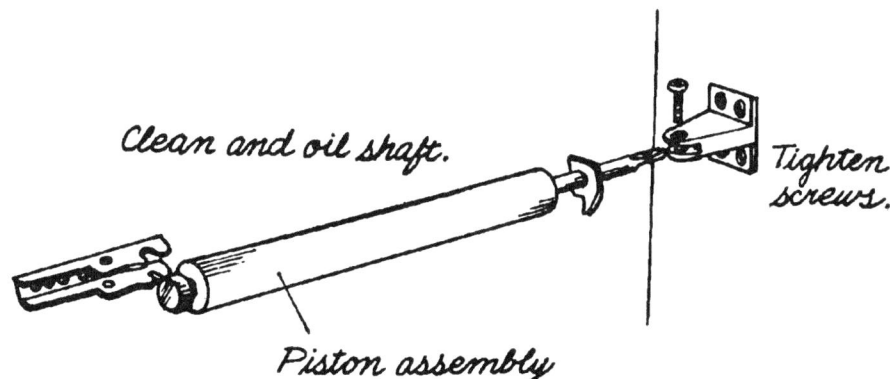

Clean and oil shaft.

Tighten screws.

Piston assembly

the opener to wear out and fail. Apply a light coating of white grease (lithium) to the rod to prevent rust and lubricate the seal. Give the mounting brackets at each end of the plunger unit a couple of drops of lightweight household oil. Wipe away any excess oil because it attracts dirt.

All mounting screws of the door closer should be tight. If the screws become loose, they will eventually enlarge their holes in the wood and fall out. To secure a loose screw, remove it, then dip a wooden match in wood glue and force it into the screw hole. Break off the match and then reinsert the screw.

If the door closes too slowly or too fast, adjust the screw in the end of the piston assembly located at the opposite end of the rod. Turn this screw counterclockwise to allow the air to escape faster, enabling the door to close faster; turn the screw clockwise to slow the air release, allowing the door to close slower. Adjust the screw so that the door closes slowly yet has enough momentum to close completely.

DOOR HINGE

The old saying that "the squeaky wheel gets the most oil" is true for a door hinge. A few drops of light machine oil whenever you notice that it is getting stiff or squeaks is all that's needed. Wipe away any excess oil because it attracts and holds dirt.

When you oil the hinge, check the hinge screws. Tighten them if any are loose. If you allow them to work loose, eventually they will fall out and the door will begin to stick or be difficult to open and close.

DRAIN

Opening a clogged drain is a real nuisance but preventing a clog is easy. Stopped-up drains usually develop over a long period of time. Accumulations of hair, soap scum, etc., gradually build up, choking off the drain opening. Once the pipe begins to fill up, the water runs slower, encouraging the clog to form even faster.

Prevent clogs in a bathtub or shower stall drain by regularly removing hair and soap scum from around the drain opening and plug. If there isn't a strainer on the drain, purchase one to fit the drain opening. These strainers come in different sizes, so measure the diameter of the opening at the drain before you go to a plumbing supplier or hardware store. Large mat-type strainers are effective and fit over any size drain.

To keep your kitchen and bathroom drains smelling sweet, periodically pour 1/4 cup of baking soda down the drain followed by a steady stream of hot water.

DRAWERS

Drawers operate by sliding along wood runners or metal tracks along the sides or bottom of a dresser or cabinet. To keep them sliding freely requires a minimum of maintenance. **Periodically** remove drawers and use the crevice tool of your vacuum to suck out dust balls, especially those that accumulate in corners.

Drawers of solid wood furniture often stick during humid weather because the wood cells absorb moisture and swell up. If you have new furniture, the inside of the drawers and casement may not be sealed. You can minimize the effect of climate on the furniture if you apply a coat of sealer or wipe-on finish to the inside and outside of the drawers during the dry season. The sealer will help prevent the wood from absorbing excess moisture during the more humid seasons.

To help eliminate friction between the drawer and its guides, lubricate both surfaces with a stub of an old wax candle. Rub this along both the drawer bottom and the wooden drawer guides. (If you use a scented candle, you'll have a pleasing aroma every time you open the drawer.) Another choice is to rub all adjoining surfaces with a silicone lubricating stick, available in hardware stores.

To maintain drawers with metal tracks, follow the same procedure for removing dust and dirt so they'll operate freely. If you find light grease already inside the mechanism of the tracks, don't wipe it up; clean around but don't remove it.

To keep drawers in a cabinet straight and square, check that the furniture is resting on a level floor. Put a carpenter's level on the top of the cabinet and check for levelness. If it's not, use shims (pieces of wood placed under the raised leg) to fill the gap.

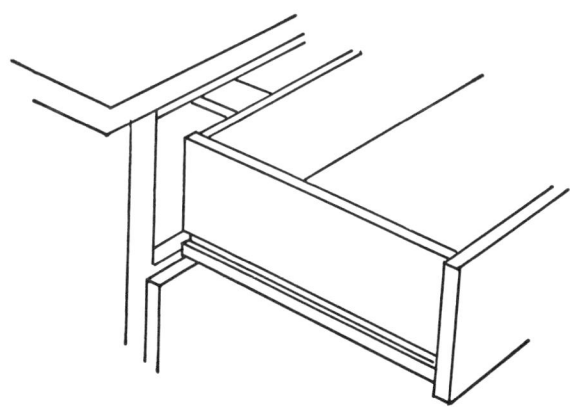

Lubricate drawer guides with candle wax.

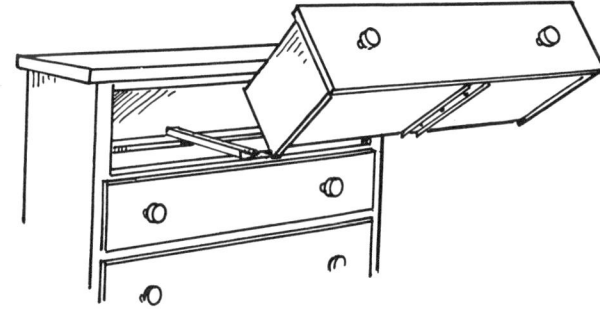

Lubricate center guide and bottom of outside edges of drawers.

DRILL, Cordless/Rechargeable

The motor of a cordless drill is a sealed unit. There is nothing that needs to be done to maintain it but the batteries do require some care in order to be able to deliver full power for an extended time. NiCad (nickel-cadmium) batteries can be recharged hundreds of times, but in order to extend their life they must be treated properly.

In general, a rechargeable battery operates best in moderate temperatures between 50 and 80 degrees. Avoid charging the batteries if they are very cold. NiCad batteries last longer if they are stored in a cool location (above freezing).

When recharging the batteries, use only the charger and charge rates specified by the manufacturer. If the drill has a built-in battery, use only the charger supplied by the manufacturer. If the battery pack is removable, recharge the battery in the proper charger; don't use one from another company.

The newer NiCad batteries have less of a memory than the older types so you don't have to completely discharge the tool before you recharge it. You should occasionally fully discharge the tool by letting it run down until it stops, in order to assure that you retain full battery capacity. Fully charge the battery before you store your drill for a long period of time.

When the tool wears out, don't throw it (or any rechargeable tool) into the garbage because it will end up in a landfill. NiCad batteries are a major source of heavy metal pollution in municipal landfills. Check with the tool manufacturer to see if the battery can be replaced. If not, take the tool and battery to a local recycling center for disposal.

DRILL, Electric

The $^3/8$-inch electric drill is usually the workhorse of the tool bench and requires more preventive maintenance than routine care. Keep dust and grit from accumulating in the drill's internal parts by directing a shot of air into its air intake port. An air hose with a nozzle attachment is the best tool for this job, but a shop vacuum with the hose placed in the blower side of the motor can also be used. Use the crevice tool attachment of the vacuum to increase the air velocity.

When you use the drill, always use sharp bits and accessories. Make the job appropriate to the tool; don't expect a consumer-grade drill to do the work of a professional-grade one. If you use a long extension cord, make sure that it is heavy enough —14 AWG (American Wire Gauge) or more—in order to carry enough current to the tool without a significant drop in line voltage.

The drill's chuck holds the bit and gets plenty of wear. A worn chuck will not hold a drill bit securely and can slip, making it difficult to drill large diameter holes. You have to overtighten the chuck to stop the slippage, which can cause the chuck to jam tight or to become very difficult to loosen when you want to change bits.

Replacement chucks are sold in hardware stores and are not difficult to install. If the drill is reversible, remove the lock screw from the center

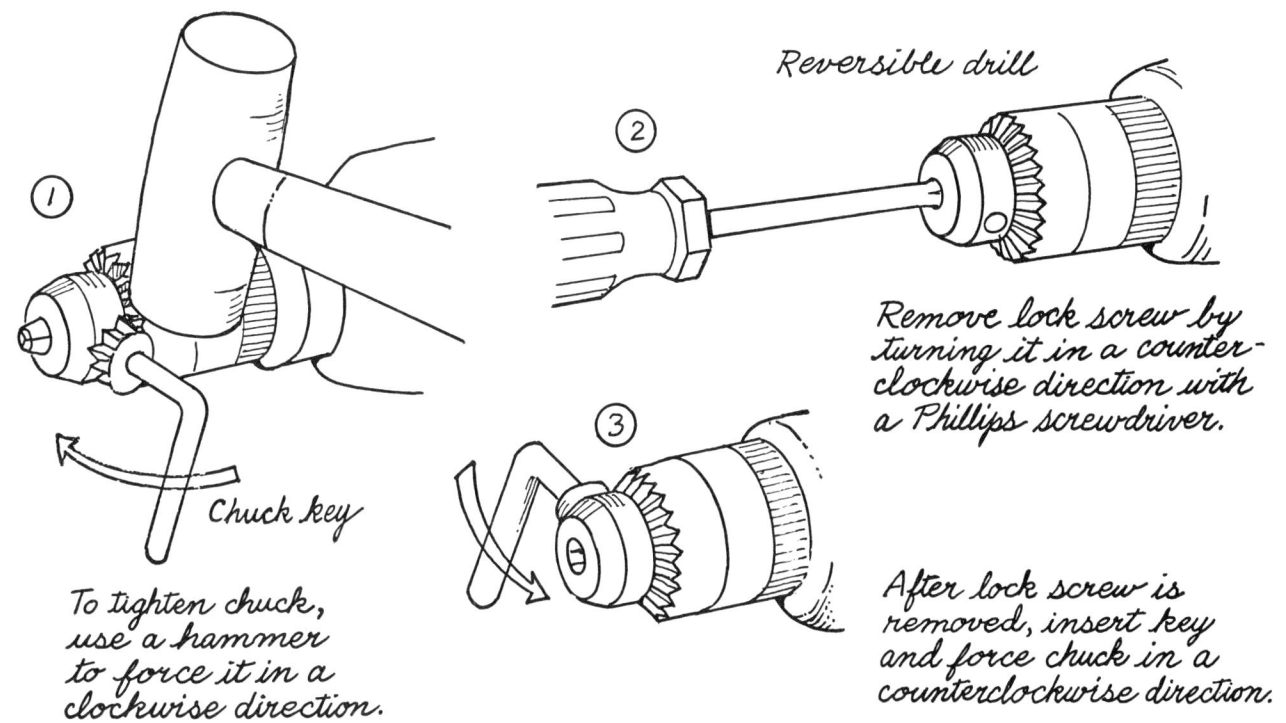

Reversible drill

① Chuck key

To tighten chuck, use a hammer to force it in a clockwise direction.

② Remove lock screw by turning it in a counter-clockwise direction with a Phillips screwdriver.

③ After lock screw is removed, insert key and force chuck in a counterclockwise direction.

of the chuck. It is easier to loosen this screw if you first tighten the chuck by placing the key in it and hitting it once with a hammer to force the chuck in a clockwise direction. Then remove the lock screw with a Phillips screwdriver. Insert the key into the chuck and hit it with a hammer, forcing the chuck

to turn in a counterclockwise direction.

Whenever you use the drill, wear safety goggles to protect your eyes from anything that might kick up from the work area into your face. When the drill is not in use, store it out of direct sunlight in a cool dry location.

FAN, Ceiling

Rotating ceiling fans have large slow-turning motors that require little care. Some units have provisions for oiling the bearings; others are sealed or saturated with oil. Check your owner's manual.

Since the fan blades collect dust and dirt, they should be cleaned **at least once a season.** Vacuum as much of the dust away with the brush attachment of a vacuum, then wipe the blades with a soft damp cloth. Also, vacuum the motor assembly.

A large accumulation of dirt or other debris on the upper side of the blades can throw them out of balance. If you notice that the fan is shaking more than usual, clean the blades. If the shaking doesn't stop, tape a metal washer or a coin to the top of one of the blades. If the shaking gets worse, move the washer or coin to another blade. Experiment until the fan runs smoothly. Then glue the washer (or washers, if necessary) in place. A smooth-turning fan will last longer because there is less stress on the motor bearings.

FAN, Exhaust

An exhaust fan in a kitchen or bathroom removes hot air, humidity, and food odors. As it pulls air outside, dirt and grease go along and settle on the grill of the fan. They will also accumulate on the fan blades or rotor cage, causing it to get out of balance and vibrate. This makes the fan noisy and also causes premature motor wear. Keeping the grill and fan clean goes a long way to operating it smoothly for a long time.

Both wall- and ceiling-mounted exhaust fans can be easily taken apart for cleaning. Do this whenever an accumulation of grease or dirt is noticeable or **at least once a year.** The time it takes for your fan to get noticeably dirty will vary, depending on how frequently you use the fan and how clean the air is.

Turn the power source to the fan "off" before you do any work on the unit. To make sure that the power is turned off at the fuse panel, run the fan and open the circuit breakers at the main panel until the fan stops. This will ensure that all power is turned off leading to the unit. When you get back into the kitchen, turn the fan switch off.

Remove the fan's grill panel, which is usually held in place with a thumb screw in the center of the grill or with screws at the corners of the grill. The thumb screw can usually be twisted loose, but you may need a pliers. To unfasten screws located in the corners, use a screwdriver.

Most kitchen exhaust fans have a grease filter that can get very dirty, so it should be cleaned **periodically.** Wash the filter and grill panel in hot soapy water. Use a rag wrapped over a paint stirrer or ruler to scrub between the grill louvers. To clean between very narrow slits, work a rag back and forth between them as if it's dental floss. Using a heavy towel, thoroughly dry the grill and filter.

Dirt and dust can accumulate in two areas in the housing of the fan. Use the crevice tool of a vacuum to clean the inside of the fan housing and a rag to wipe away any dirt that has accumulated at the exterior opening of the fan.

Then wash the fan blades with a damp rag. If they are greasy, use a cleaning solution, but rinse the blades carefully and dry them completely. If the paint is nicked or the blades show signs of rust, spray them with a rust-inhibiting paint.

Reassemble the entire unit, including the filter and grill, before restoring power.

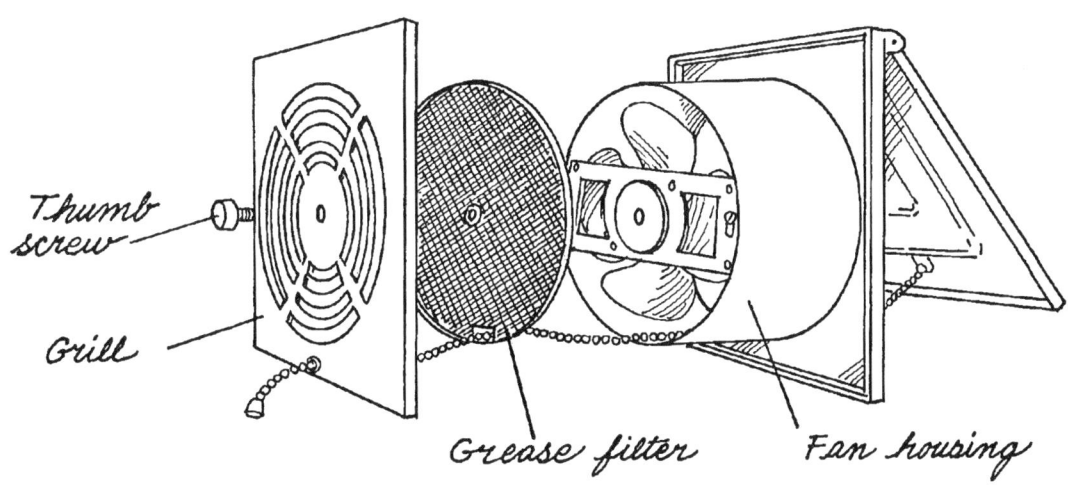

FAN, House

Very large whole house fans and older smaller models are often belt-driven. The motor is mounted on the side of the fan and a V-belt transfers power to the fan. Over time the belt stretches and needs to be tightened. Turn the fan on, then go to the service panel and open the breaker that supplies power to the fan. When the fan stops, the power has been turned off. Go back to the fan and turn its switch off. The fan is now safe to work on.

Once a year loosen the motor mounting bolts to tension the V-belt. Pull the fan motor away from the large fan pulley mounted on the fan shaft until the belt deflects (moves inward) about 1/2 inch when you push it in the center between the motor pulley and fan pulley. Then retighten the fan motor's bolts. Don't overtighten the belt or you may cause premature wear to the motor and fan shaft bearings.

Replace the V-belt if it's hardened or has small cracks, or if you can pull the motor far from the center pulley and the belt remains loose. Your owner's manual will have the part number of the V-belt. If you can't find the manual, take the old belt with you to the hardware store and get a duplicate.

At least once a year apply a few drops of light machine oil to the motor and fan shaft bearings.

41

Check the owner's manual. Some motors have permanently lubricated bearings that require no attention.

If the fan is mounted in the ceiling behind a shutter, clean and service the shutter while you are working on the fan. Vacuum all dirt or dust that has accumulated on the shutter fins and in the mechanism that connects the blades together. If the blades are sticking, spray the ends with a silicone lubricant, then work the fins back and forth until they move freely.

Most of the newer models of whole house fans are direct-drive and except for **yearly** blade cleaning they are basically maintenance-free. Check the owner's manual to see if the motor bearings should be periodically oiled.

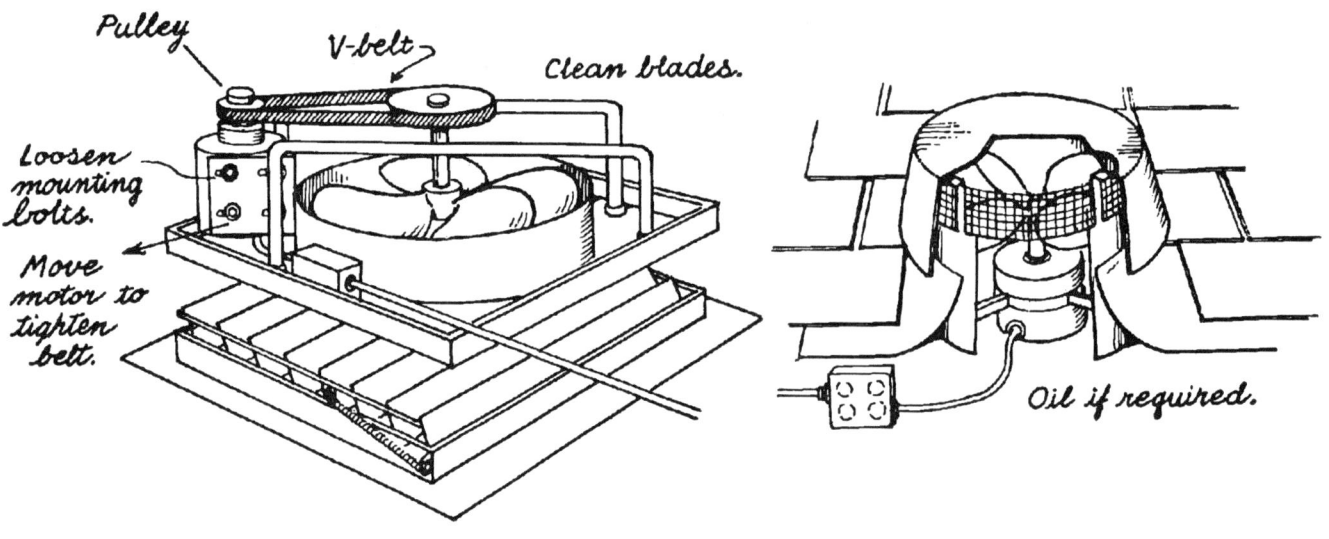

FAN, Window

Box fans or window fans should be cleaned **at the end of each season.** Unplug the fan, then remove the front or back grill. Wash the blades with water and a mild household detergent. Vacuum dust and dirt from the motor housing and from the speed control of the on/off switch.

Apply a couple of drops of lightweight machine oil to the fan shaft. You might have to remove the blade to do this because some fans have a plastic blade assembly that covers the motor. To remove the blade, loosen the nuts in the center of the blade that hold it to the motor shaft. Some fan blade assemblies are held in place by a set screw located in the side of the central hub. Loosen the set screw with a screwdriver. It may have a hex head that needs to be removed with an Allen wrench. Pull the blade assembly off the motor shaft. Oil the shaft, then replace the blade and tighten the screw.

FAUCET

If you have a single faucet for hot and cold water or there are two handles on the faucet, you probably have one that uses compression washers. These parts will stay in working order longer if you turn the faucet "on" and "off" gently. Overtightening causes excessive wear.

If the faucet has an aerator at the end of the spout to catch small particles of rust or pipe scale deposits, *periodically* check that the aerator isn't clogged. A clogged aerator will choke off the water flow to a trickle. Unscrew the aerator cap, which has a fine screen that traps sediment, and clean it.

Disassemble the parts of the faucet (see illustration); keep them in order so that you can reassemble the unit when you're finished. Clean any dirt or deposits from the screen with a pin or thin wire. To do so, hold the screen upside down in a stream of water so that the water flows through it in the opposite direction. You may also have to use a pin to clear large particles of dirt, but don't damage the screen by pushing the pin through the fine mesh screen.

Reassemble the aerator and then screw it back on the faucet. Turn the water on and test the flow. If the unit doesn't produce an even stream filled with small bubbles, you may have reassembled the unit incorrectly. If you are certain it's reassembled correctly but the flow of water is still just a trickle, the unit may be worn out.

Aerators are inexpensive, so purchase a new one. There are several gauges of threads used at the end of faucets, so bring the old unit with you when you purchase a replacement. Try attaching the old unit onto a display faucet in the store, then make sure that the new one will screw onto the same faucet. This guarantees that the new aerator will match the threads on your faucet.

To remove spotty water marks from the chrome housing of a faucet, wipe it with a rag soaked in white vinegar. When it's dry, buff the chrome with a terry cloth rag. For very dull chrome, repeat this process a few times.

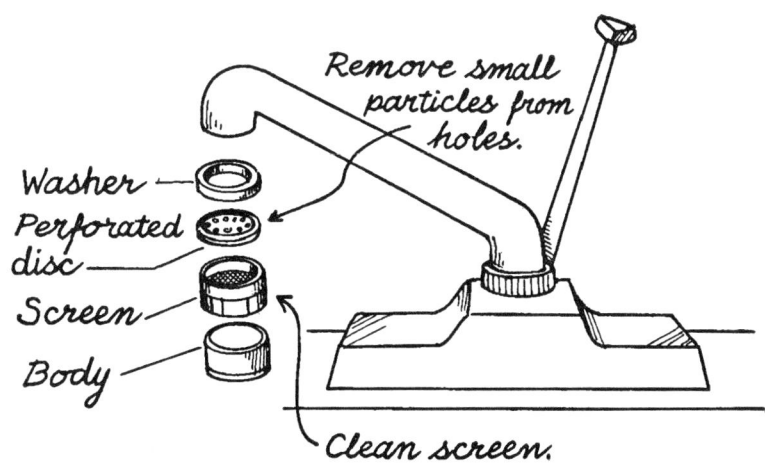

Washer
Perforated disc
Screen
Body

Remove small particles from holes.

Clean screen.

Like most electronic gadgets, a fax (facsimile) machine will work better, more reliably, and last longer if you keep it clean and feed it the right type of paper.

An inexpensive 2-inch-wide nylon paintbrush can come in handy to whisk away dust particles between the keys and push buttons.

Before replacing a roll of fax (thermal) paper, use the brush to dust out the paper chamber and around the paper cutting bar or the automatic cutter because paper lint and dust accumulate in this area. When you replace the roll of paper, always use the recommended thermal recording paper that's specified by the manufacturer. If you purchase an extra supply, store the rolls in their original unopened package in a cool dry cabinet out of direct sunlight.

Remove greasy dirt from the outside of the machine's case with a clean rag dampened with a mild soap and water solution. If dirt is in the narrow spaces between keys, dip a cotton-tipped swab in the solution, squeeze out the excess, and work the swab back and forth between the keys.

Go over the dampened surface with a dry rag or cotton swab. Don't use strong household cleaners on any of the plastic parts.

Most fax machines are left on all the time so they can receive a message anytime. These machines are vulnerable to voltage spikes on the power and telephone lines. Most manufacturers recommend that you protect your machine with a surge suppressor placed between it and the power line. In addition to this protection you can also install a surge suppressor on the telephone line. Telephone wires can also deliver a voltage spike that can damage the electronic circuits inside the fax if lightning strikes close to a nearby utility pole. Surge protectors are sold in hardware and office equipment stores.

Some machines use a long-lasting battery (usually lithium) to keep the internal memory active so it will not forget your setup conditions and recorded telephone numbers. The battery will last longer if you leave the machine on, because the memory requires battery power only when the machine is turned off.

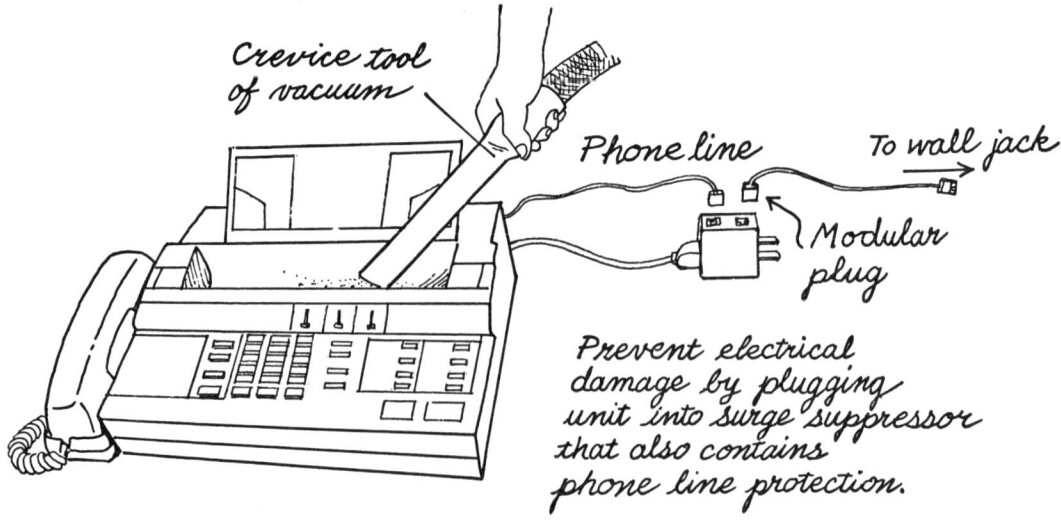

Crevice tool of vacuum

Phone line

To wall jack

Modular plug

Prevent electrical damage by plugging unit into surge suppressor that also contains phone line protection.

FIRE EXTINGUISHER

Every home should have a fire extinguisher handy. If you do but haven't looked at it in a couple of years, you may not be as prepared for an emergency as you think. A fire extinguisher is one of those devices that can hang on the wall for years unused, but when you need it, it's got to work.

Home fire extinguishers are filled with dry chemicals or Halon gas. Different types of extinguishers are designed to fight particular types of fire: class A is for wood, paper, trash, etc.; class B is for gasoline or other flammable liquids; class C is for electrical fires.

Dry chemical and Halon extinguishers should be inspected on a regular basis to assure that they will function when you pull the trigger. All types of fire extinguishers are pressurized, so there is the potential for a leak. The fire-fighting chemicals, either sodium bicarbonate (class B and C fires) or monoammonium phosphate (class A, B, and C fires) inside the extinguisher will settle and compact in the bottom of the extinguisher over time. These powders can become so compacted that they will not dispense properly even if the extinguisher has full pressure.

Every month remove the extinguisher from its mounting bracket and look at the pressure gauge to see that it is charged. The indicator should be in the green area of the dial. On some extinguishers you may have to push a test button to activate the gauge. If the pressure is low or excessive, have the extinguisher serviced by a professional.

If it's a dry chemical extinguisher, turn it upside down and shake it to loosen the dry chemical charge. Check that the lock or safety pin is in place and that there's no sign of corrosion or dents to the tank. If the extinguisher still doesn't work properly, have it recharged at a fire extinguisher recharging service center, listed in the Yellow Pages under "Fire Extinguishers."

Make sure that everyone in your family knows where the extinguisher is located and how to operate it (and to dial 911 immediately) if a fire occurs. Your local fire department should be able to provide you with further information on home emergencies and fire prevention.

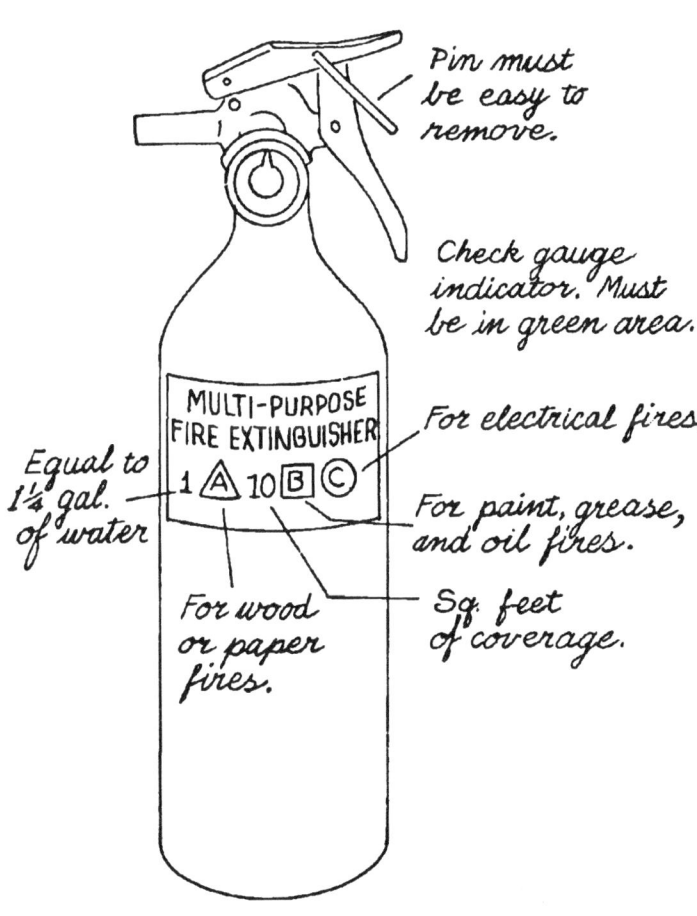

Pin must be easy to remove.

Check gauge indicator. Must be in green area.

Equal to 1¼ gal. of water

For electrical fires.

For paint, grease, and oil fires.

For wood or paper fires.

Sq. feet of coverage.

MULTI-PURPOSE FIRE EXTINGUISHER 1 Ⓐ 10 Ⓑ Ⓒ

FIREPLACE

All fireplaces require **yearly maintenance** to be safe. Chimney fires are a very real threat to your house and family if you use your fireplace regularly and don't have the chimney cleaned. Hire a chimney sweep to remove the buildup of creosote on the interior walls of your chimney **each spring or summer.** (Look in your local Yellow Pages under "Chimney.") If you want to clean the chimney on your own, see page 22 for how-to advice. Even if you don't use the fireplace much, your chimney should be cleaned every couple of years.

When you use the fireplace, sweep up the ashes from previous fires that have settled beneath the grate to assure better air flow for a faster-starting fire. Keep a small broom and dustpan specifically for this purpose near the fireplace. Store newspapers, kindling, and firewood nearby (but not so close that they might catch on fire) to avoid making a mess when transferring them to the firebox.

Use a fireproof hearth carpet to catch stray sparks that may shoot beyond the screen and damage the carpet or floor (and possibly start a fire).

Always operate a fireplace with the chimney in the open position. When not in use, close it to keep out cold drafts and to keep pests (squirrels, birds) from entering the house down the chimney.

Check to see that the grate which holds the firewood is stable. If it's wobbly, see if one of the bolts holding the leg in place needs tightening. If that's not the cause, buy a replacement grate of similar size.

When the fireplace is not in use, thoroughly clean the fireplace hearth and surrounding area. Protect the area around the fireplace by laying down an old sheet or drop cloth. Sweep out ashes with a small dust broom and pan or a heavy-duty shop vacuum. Use the crevice tool of a vacuum to remove dust from cracks and corners. If there is a clean-out pit at the bottom of the chimney (in the basement or crawl space), empty it.

Remove any unused firewood, kindling, and newspapers, and store them outside.

FLUORESCENT LIGHT

Because fluorescent tubes are so energy-efficient and long-lasting they are becoming more popular in today's homes. Fluorescent bulbs last up to 20,000 hours, but as they age their light output (lumens) decreases. Replace a fluorescent bulb **every two years or so, or when dimming or flickering is noticeable.**

Fluorescent tubes last so long that they collect considerable amounts of dust. To keep these lights working at peak efficiency, dust the fixture tubes, defuser, and reflector **regularly.**

FREEZER, Self-defrosting

Periodically let the food supply in the freezer dwindle down so that it can be emptied and cleaned. Turn the appliance off and unplug the unit. Clean the interior of the freezer with a solution of baking soda and water. Use a mild soap and water to wash the rubber door gasket. If food particles are lodged in the grooves of the gasket, spread the grooves apart and use a soft toothbrush to remove debris. Wipe the interior dry.

Use a crevice tool fitted to your vacuum or a long-handled brush (such as one you use to remove snow from your car's windshield) to dust off the condensing coils located at the bottom or back of the freezer. Dust and lint caught in these coils restrict the air flow and reduce the efficiency of the unit.

The freezer should be turned "on" for at least an hour before it is filled with food.

FURNACE

Most new homes and many older homes are heated with a furnace. This system transfers heat—created by burning gas, oil, or coal, or by heating a resistance element with electricity—to air that is circulated throughout the house. The furnace itself is designed to be trouble-free and requires very little care, but the gas or oil burner that creates the heat does require maintenance to run safely and efficiently. *(General maintenance tips for most types of furnaces are given in this entry. See the separate entries for electric, gas, and oil furnaces, which contain more detailed information on servicing their burners.)*

The best time of year to service a furnace is *in the fall*, before the heating season begins. The only tools you need are a flashlight and a household vacuum with a hose attachment. Start by inspecting the outside of the furnace. Look carefully at the flue pipe leading from the furnace to the chimney. Check for loose connections wherever two pipes join, at all elbows, and where the pipe joins the chimney. If you see loose sections of pipe, push the parts together. Also check for large rust spots, especially on the bottom of the pipes. Condensation may cause rusting and this is a sure sign of a maladjusted burner. If you find large rust spots, or loose or missing cement surrounding the pipe where it enters the chimney, call your furnace repair service and have it repaired professionally.

All furnaces have some sort of air filter. Most are located in the return air duct system, usually at the bottom of the furnace where the large duct enters the furnace. This filter should be replaced *regularly,* unless it is a permanent foam-type filter.

Replaceable furnace filters come in many sizes and can be purchased from most hardware stores, lumberyards, and home centers. *In the spring,* purchase a supply of these filters when they go on sale. If you have central air conditioning, you will need to replace these filters *monthly.*

To change a filter all you have to do is slide the old filter out and replace it with a clean filter. The

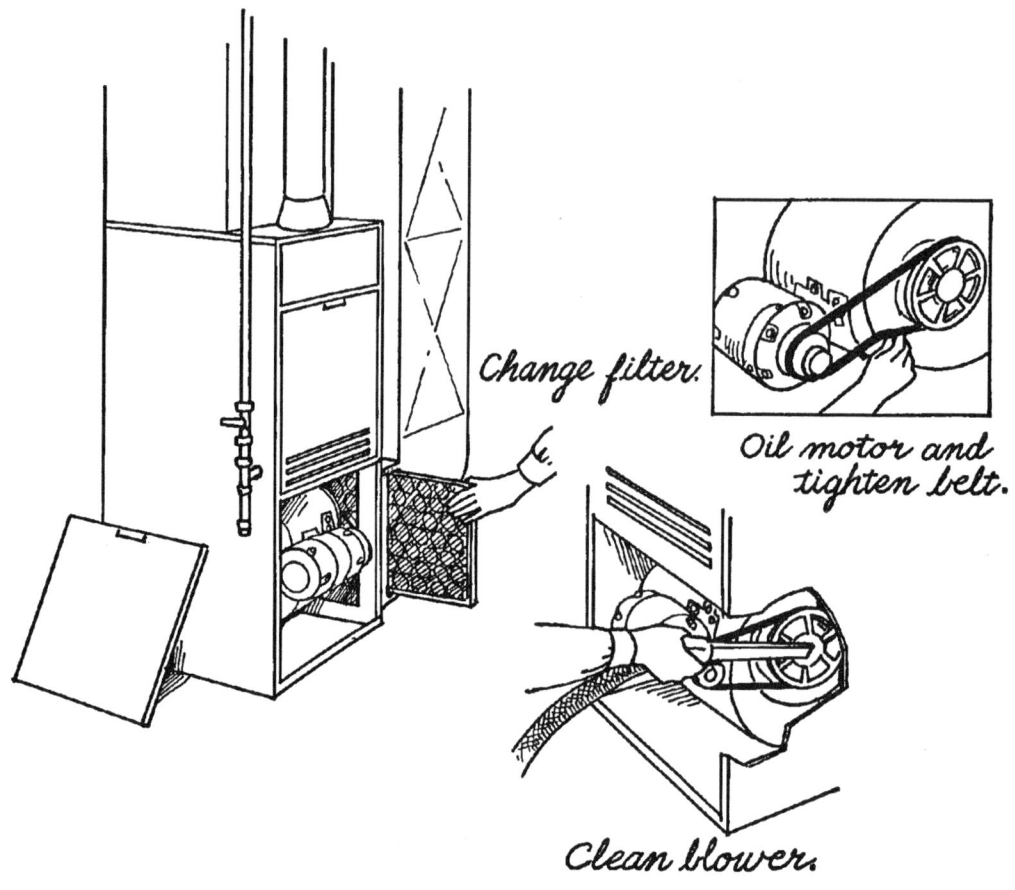

Change filter.

Oil motor and
tighten belt.

Clean blower.

filter is clearly marked, showing how to insert it into the furnace so that the correct side faces the incoming air.

Your furnace may have a U-shaped hammock filter, located at the bottom of the furnace below the blower assembly. To get at it you have to remove an inspection panel from the side of the furnace. This filter can be removed by lifting the wire frame off its rack and pushing it together; then pull the filter directly out of the furnace.

The filter element will most likely be made out of fiberglass and can be purchased at hardware stores or home centers. Remove the old filter and throw it away or cut a new piece of filter material from the roll and wrap it around the wire frame.

Both flat and hammock filters may have a permanent filter element (made of foam or other material) that can be cleaned and reused. Remove the filter and give it a good vacuuming, then wash it in warm water and a mild detergent. Check with the manufacturer of your particular furnace for specific cleaning instructions.

A furnace has a blower that forces the air through the heating system. Some blowers have a V-belt drive that should be serviced *every year.* Some newer furnaces have direct drive blowers and are not belt-driven. Both systems require cleaning and a little oil.

The furnace blower is usually located in the bottom of a typical upright furnace right behind the furnace filter. There is an access panel in the side of the furnace that opens up or comes off to expose the blower assembly.

MAKE SURE THAT THE POWER IS TURNED OFF TO THE FURNACE AT YOUR MAIN CIRCUIT PANEL. The blower is controlled by the thermostat. If the power is not turned off and someone turns up the thermostat while you have your head in the furnace, the blower will begin to operate and cause you severe injury. The furnace is safe to work on only AFTER THE POWER IS TURNED OFF.

On most belt-drive blower assemblies both the blower motor shaft and the fan shaft require oiling *once a year.* If you see small spouts with little covers on them at either end of the motor or blower shafts, you should oil the unit. Fill the oil cups with 20-weight machine oil, but don't over-oil because the excess will run out and collect dirt. Direct-drive units may or may not require oil; consult your owner's manual for specific directions.

If there is a drive or V-belt, inspect it for cracks or frayed areas. Replace it if it looks at all suspicious because it is an inexpensive item. If the belt fails some cold night, an emergency service call may become an expensive reality. Loosen the hold-down bolts that secure the motor assembly, and push the motor toward the blower to slacken the belt. Many furnaces have printed instructions on how to change the belt on the inside of the removable panel.

Remove the V-belt and take it to your local hardware store or home center and purchase a replacement. Reinstall the belt in the reverse order that you removed it. Check that the tension is correct. If you push the belt in the center between the pulleys, it should deflect at least $1/2$ inch. Don't overtighten the belt as this may cause excessive wear in the motor or blower.

If the furnace is equipped with a humidifier, it requires *at least yearly maintenance. (See the entry for "Humidifier, Furnace unit.")*

FURNACE, Electric

Electric furnaces are extremely efficient and the actual heating elements have no moving parts. Besides *yearly maintenance* outlined in the previous entry, there is not much you can do to keep the furnace operating efficiently.

Electricity is an expensive fuel, and even though an electric furnace is efficient, dirt and dust in the system will cut down its efficiency. Regularly clean the registers in each room with the crevice tool of a vacuum to remove dust balls and dirt. Dirty registers that are partially blocked with a buildup of dirt will restrict the amount of air that can pass through the duct, which in turn lowers the efficiency of your furnace and costs you money.

FURNACE, Gas

Gas furnaces run cleanly and their burners require minimal maintenance. Besides **yearly maintenance,** outlined on pages 47–49, a major tune-up of the gas burner assembly should be done by a professional.

There are several easy maintenance procedures that you can safely perform that will go a long way toward keeping your furnace in top shape. MAKE SURE THAT THE POWER IS TURNED OFF TO THE FURNACE AT YOUR MAIN CIRCUIT PANEL. The gas burner and furnace blower are controlled by the thermostat. If the power is not turned off to the furnace and someone turns up the thermostat, the burner will light and could severely injure you. Turn off the circuit breaker serving the furnace before you start any maintenance work.

The gas burners are located in the central portion of the furnace. The front panel will usually

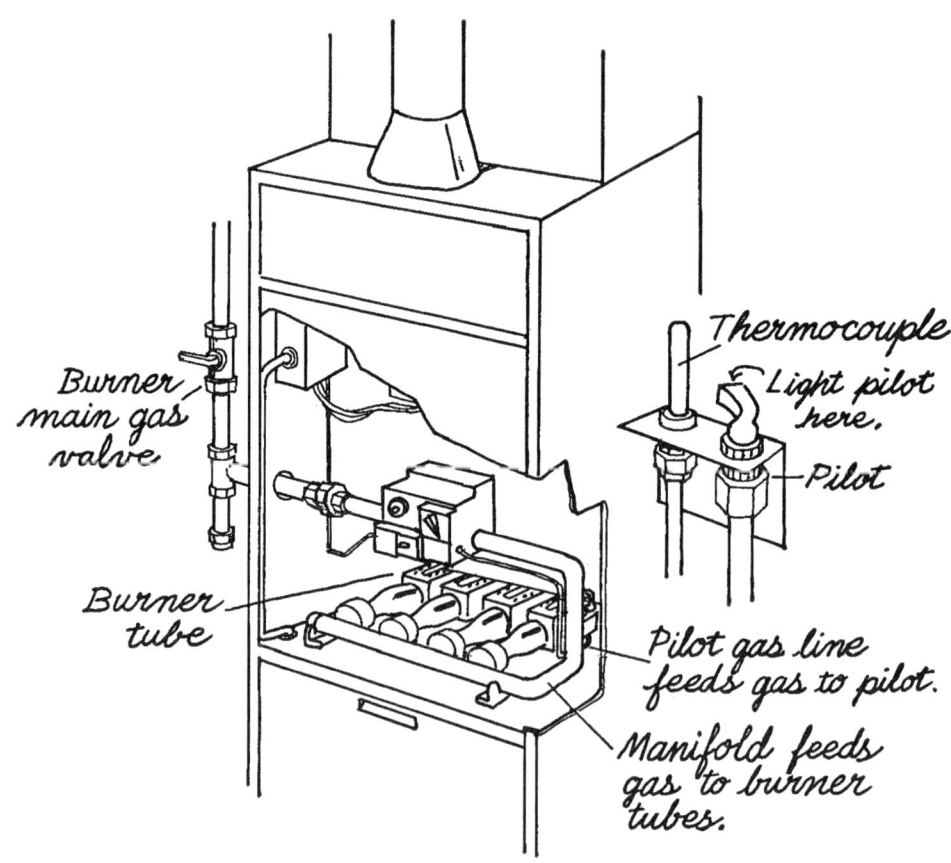

Burner main gas valve

Burner tube

Thermocouple

Light pilot here.

Pilot

Pilot gas line feeds gas to pilot.

Manifold feeds gas to burner tubes.

lift off to expose a row of horizontal tubes. Check the owner's manual for specific directions to remove this panel.

The burner tubes lead inside the furnace and are part of the burner assembly, which is basically the same as that of a gas stove, only the burner tubes are larger. Along the top of these tubes are the burner heads with small holes through which the gas-air mixture passes to be burned. With the crevice tool of your vacuum, remove any flaking rust particles or other debris from the top of the burner heads. Dirt will block the small holes and prevent the burners from operating efficiently. Also, vacuum any dirt under the burner assembly and any debris from the front openings of the burner tubes.

Don't try to adjust any of the safety controls yourself; have the furnace professionally inspected and tuned up *every couple of years.* A properly adjusted gas burner will save you money in the long run.

FURNACE, Oil

An oil furnace is a rather complicated piece of machinery and requires regular maintenance to keep it working efficiently. Servicing the many controls and safety sensors on an oil furnace should be left to a trained oil burner service technician. An *annual fall tune-up* will pay for itself over the next heating season because an oil burner out-of-tune can be not only inefficient but costly. MAKE SURE BEFORE DOING ANY WORK THAT THE POWER TO THE FURNACE IS TURNED OFF AT YOUR MAIN CIRCUIT PANEL.

Following are some maintenance procedures that you can safely perform to keep an oil furnace in good working condition. First and foremost, keep the burner clean and free of dirt. An oil burner digests large amounts of air that are used in combustion which, in turn, cause the burner housing to get oily and attract dirt. If the air intake port becomes partially blocked, the burner will not operate efficiently and you will lose precious heat up the chimney in the form of excess smoke. Keep the burner housing clean with a vacuum crevice tool and also keep the air intake ports clear.

Once a year put a few drops of 30-weight machine oil in the oil cups located at the end of the burner motor. However, since over-oiling can damage the motor, don't do this if a service technician oils the motor during a yearly tune-up.

Changing the fuel oil filter is another job that is messy but not difficult. Look on the top of the filter housing and record the name of the filter and the model number. Call a local heating oil supplier or burner service to see if they have a filter element. If they don't have that particular model number, ask them to recommend a comparable filter element. Make sure that you find a suitable replacement element before you take it apart.

Replacing the filter element is easy. Turn off the oil supply with the valve at the bottom of the tank. Place a bucket under the filter and loosen the bolt in the center of the filter top. Some filters have a bolt at the bottom of the filter bowl. Use an adjustable or open-end wrench to loosen it. If the bolt is very tight, hold the body of the filter to prevent it from twisting and bending the copper lines connected to the filter. When the bolt is

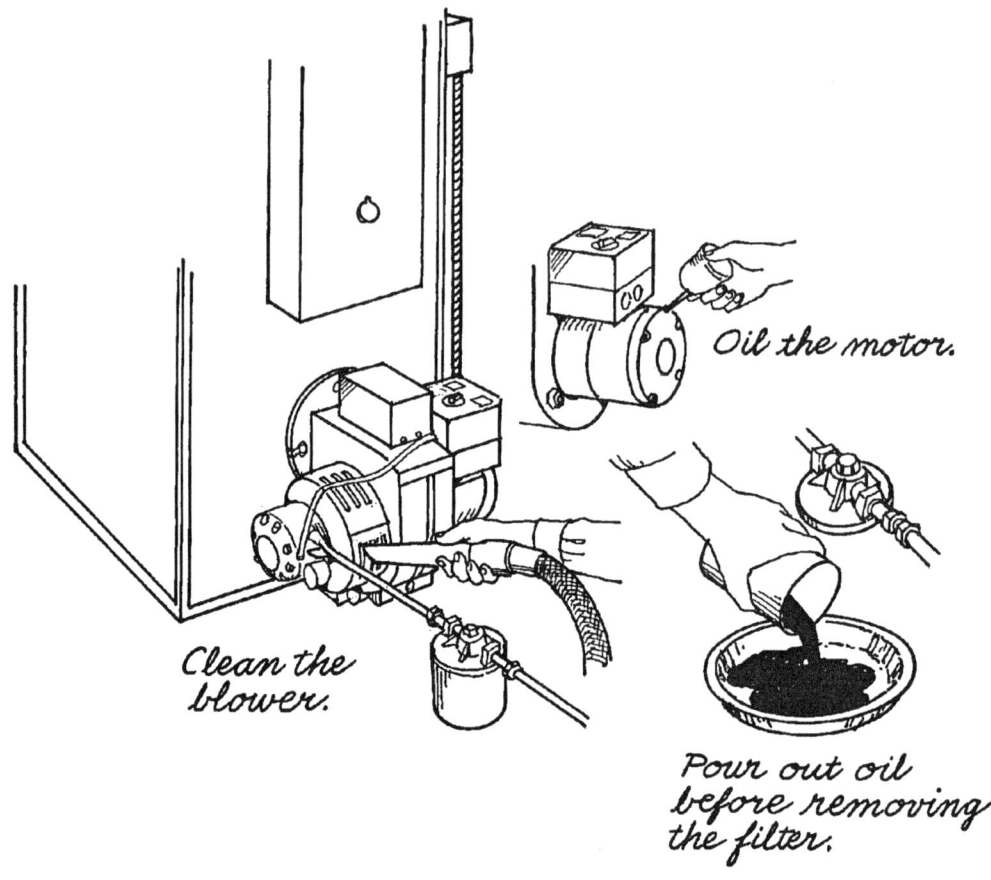

Oil the motor.

Clean the blower.

Pour out oil before removing the filter.

loosened, the bottom of the filter will drop off. Some older styles may have a T handle that you turn to loosen the top.

Dump the oil in the filter bowl into the bucket and remove the old filter element. Replace the element, then soak the new gasket in oil and replace the gasket around the top of the filter bowl. Reassemble the unit.

Next, bleed the air out of the system. Open the small bolt on the top of the filter and turn on the oil. Wait until you see some oil start to run out of the bolt hole, then tighten the bolt. If the top of the filter comes off, leave it on loosely until oil starts to

leak out around the top; then tighten the T handle to seal up the filter.

Turn the power back on to the furnace and turn up the thermostat to fire up the burner. It should start to fire right away, but the furnace may shut down if a small amount of air gets into the burner system. If it does, push the reset button on the relay box and try again. When the burner fires up, let it run for a few minutes—even if it's warm outside—to make sure that all the air is out of the system. After about five minutes, turn the thermostat down so that the oil burner goes off, turning off the furnace.

Most automatic door openers manufactured after 1982 are equipped with contact-reversing and 30-second reversing capability. That means if the bottom of the door touches someone or something as it's going down, it will automatically reverse its direction. To test this, place a two-inch-thick block of wood on the ground under the open garage door. If the door doesn't reverse when it hits the wood, disconnect the opener and either have it repaired or replaced.

Check your owner's manual or call a local dealer who sells your make of garage door for specific details on maintenance or follow these general guidelines.

At least once a year look at the door springs, cables rollers, and pulleys of your garage door to check for fraying and other damage. If you see any damage, call a professional garage door dealer; don't try to adjust the door springs or hardware yourself.

Check the balance of the door springs ***twice a year.*** Disengage the opener and manually lower the door. When it gets to your waist, release the door. It should remain in place and not move up or down. If it does move, the springs need to be adjusted by a professional garage door dealer. Don't try to do this yourself because the springs are under tension and can cause serious injury if mishandled.

To see if the door cables are fraying, run a rag along the cable; it will catch on any broken or frayed wires. If it catches or tears the rag, the cable should be checked by a professional.

Lubricate the drive mechanism that raises and

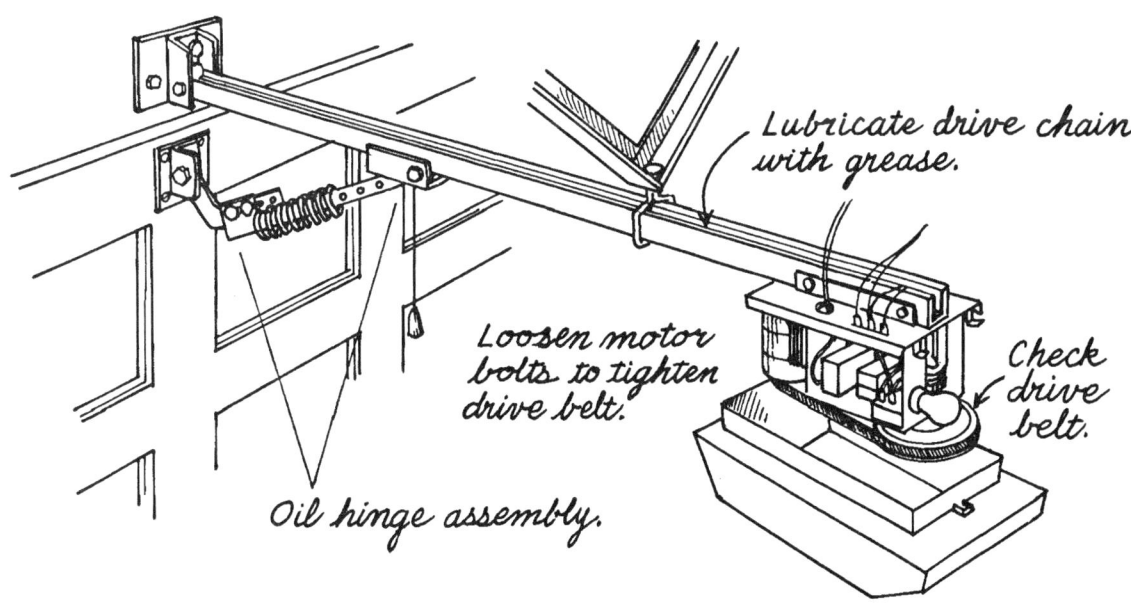

Lubricate drive chain with grease.

Loosen motor bolts to tighten drive belt.

Check drive belt.

Oil hinge assembly.

lowers the door with a light grease recommended by the door manufacturer or a white lithium grease. The unit will have either a chain or screw drive and both should receive a light coating of grease. Also oil the door arm at all pivot points.

If the unit is equipped with a drive belt, check that it is not worn or frayed. Replace it if it's worn.

If the belt is slipping or squeaks during operation, tighten it. On most units equipped with a drive belt you can tighten the belt by loosening the bolts holding the electric motor in place and pulling the motor away from the large drive pulley while tightening the motor bolts. If the belt keeps slipping or squeaks, replace it.

GARAGE DOOR, Manual swing-up

Overhead garage doors are trouble-free if they are given basic maintenance. Timely lubrication is the most important step in maintaining a one-piece swing-up door.

Swing-up garage doors have large pivot hinges at each side, located about midway up the door jamb (side post). *At least once a year* lubricate these hinges and all moving hardware with a light all-purpose grease.

Check the mounting bolts and hardware on the door for any loose or missing screws. Replace them as soon as possible to prevent the adjacent screws from also working loose. If the screw has worked out, repair the door by drilling completely through it and replacing the screw with the same sized nut, washer, and bolt. A nut and bolt combination is stronger than a screw and will hold the hinge firmly in place even if some of the other mounting screws are beginning to work loose.

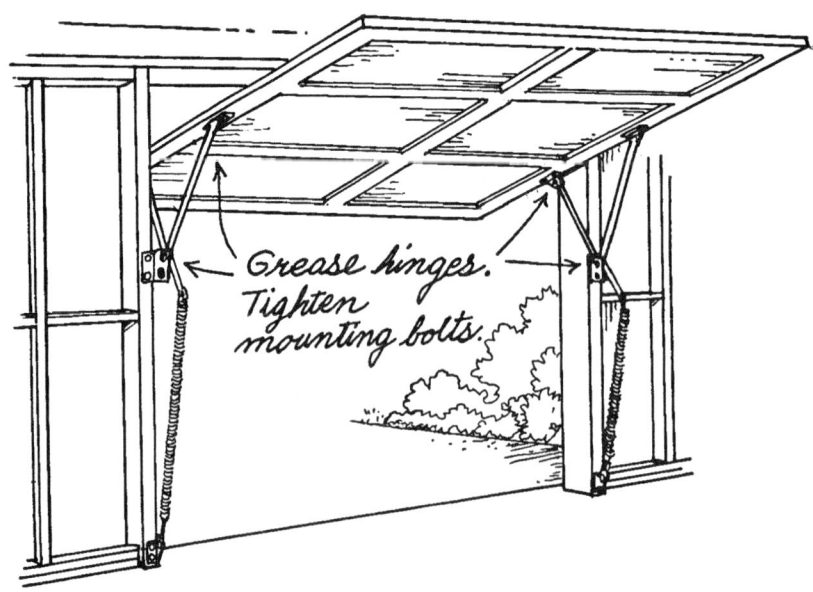

Grease hinges.
Tighten mounting bolts.

GARAGE DOOR, Overhead segmented roll-up

An overhead segmented or sectional garage door is trouble-free if it receives basic maintenance, which means checking to see that all the rollers are kept well oiled. If a roller wheel becomes stiff and difficult to operate, it creates friction between it and the track, which in turn causes strain on the system. You have to push on the door harder and eventually the tracks get out of line.

At least once a year or whenever the door is difficult to operate, lubricate with 20-weight oil the hinges connecting the door segments, the rollers, and any other moving hardware.

After lubricating the door, open and close it several times. If you feel any binding in the track,

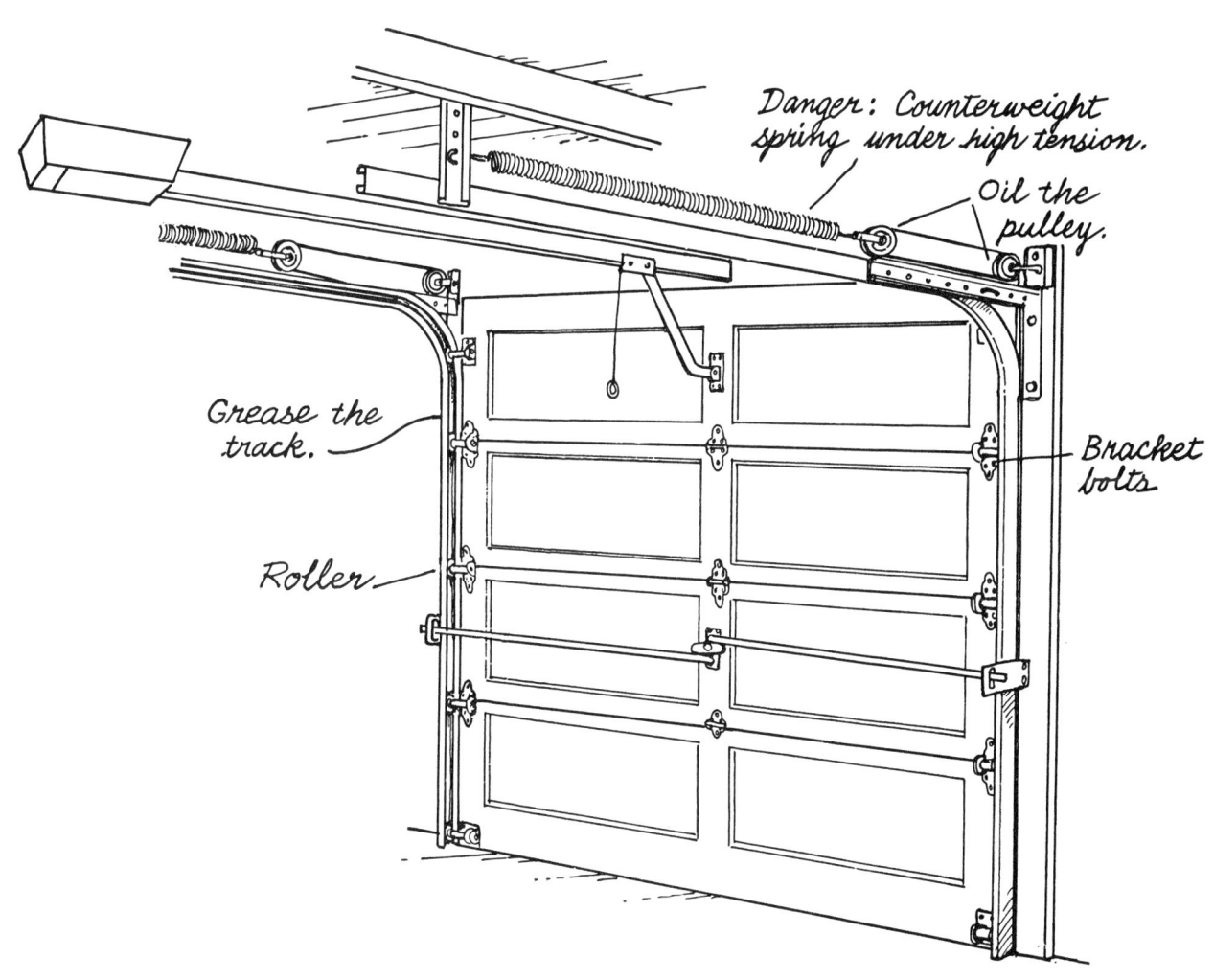

Danger: Counterweight spring under high tension.

Oil the pulley.

Grease the track.

Roller

Bracket bolts

check for bent rollers or a misaligned track.

A roller may become so stiff and difficult to turn that its shaft bends; then it begins to jam in the track, which causes more friction and bending. Have someone open and close the door while you look for bent roller shafts and rollers that stick and don't turn.

You can usually loosen a sticking roller with a couple of squirts of household oil, but replace any rollers that have bent shafts. Replacement parts for overhead doors can be purchased at most large hardware stores and home centers. All these parts are held to the door with bolts and replacement is easy.

If you do find sticking rollers or rollers with bent shafts, you should also check the door track alignment. First, replace the bad rollers or be sure that all are rolling smoothly, then open and close the door and feel if the door is binding.

If you do feel the door binding in a particular area as you lift it, have a helper hold the door in that position while you check the track where the rollers of the top door segment are located. These rollers should be centered in the track, not touching its sides.

The track alignment can be adjusted by loosening the bracket bolts that secure the mounting hardware to the door jamb. Open the door all the way and then loosen the bolts just enough so that the track brackets can move in and out (the mounting holes are slots). If the rollers are binding on the inside of the track, place a piece of scrap wood against the outside of the track at the nearest mounting bracket and hit the wood to move the track in. A slight adjustment is all that is needed. Then recheck the track and roller alignment. Tighten the bolts and test the door action. If it binds somewhere else, make the necessary adjustments.

If the door is wood, keep it painted inside and out to resist water and to prevent warping damage. Also, keep snow, ice, and leaves cleared away from the area surrounding the garage door so that it can open and close freely. Check for loose weather stripping mounted on the door jamb and along the bottom. If it's loose, reinstall it; if it's worn away, replace it.

Another area that requires periodic maintenance is the bottom of the door. This area should be kept painted and the weather stripping maintained so that the door can't absorb water along its bottom edge and begin to delaminate or rot. If the weather stripping is worn, purchase a new roll of weather stripping along with galvanized roofing nails to install it. Installation is easy: just nail it in place, but before you do, give the bottom of the door a fresh coat of exterior paint.

GARBAGE DISPOSAL

There are two basic types of garbage disposals. The continuous-feed type is started by a switch near the sink and operates continuously as you run the water and feed in the waste garbage. A batch-feed unit is first loaded with garbage and then the top is secured, which starts the disposal running. Either type will run trouble-free unless you overload it or abuse it in some other way.

To prevent jamming the unit, fill it halfway with loose pieces of garbage instead of packing it full. Check your owner's manual for the types of food you should not put in a garbage disposal. Usually fibrous or stringy foods like artichokes or banana peels should not be put into a disposal.

If the disposal clogs or stops operating, turn off the electricity to the unit. Dislodge the clog with the end of a wooden spoon or broomstick. Don't reach into the disposal with your hand.

If the motor stops because of a clog or from overloading, look for the red reset button at the bottom or side of the disposal motor, which is located under the sink. Press in the reset button until you hear a click. Turn the power on to the unit and activate the unit.

You can keep a garbage disposal odor-free by throwing in half a lemon or orange, **once a month,** and then running the unit with warm water.

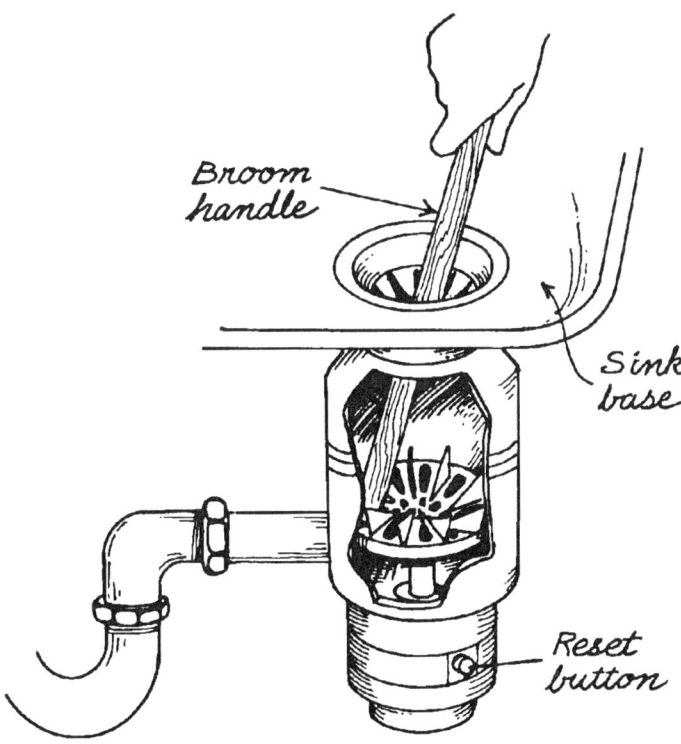

GUTTER / DOWNSPOUT

Clean gutters and downspouts **twice a year** and they will protect your house from water damage almost forever. To remove fallen leaves and dirt that accumulate in the gutters, you need a sturdy ladder, two buckets with a rope, work gloves, and a helper. With one person working on the ladder, filling an empty bucket with debris, and the other person disposing of the debris, the task goes quickly. The second bucket lets the person on the ladder continue working his or her way around the house.

When the gutters are free of debris, use a garden hose (or several sections of them) to flush out the dirt and to make sure that rainwater can run through the gutters to the downspouts. While doing this, check for leaks that should be patched. Also check to see that the straps that hold the gutters and downspouts in place are secure. If they are loose, reinstall or replace them.

If during the winter months a heavy buildup of snow settles on the roof near the gutters, try to dislodge it. If you can reach the area safely, use a broom to remove the snow or large icicles so that they don't weigh down the gutters and bend them.

HAIR DRYER

Hair dryers get extremely hot inside, in fact they're designed to do just that. Cool air is pulled into the back of the unit where it's warmed, and it comes out the front end of the unit as hot blasts of air. The flow of air through the dryer cools the inside and prevents the dryer from overheating.

To keep a "gun"-type hand-held hair dryer working, it is essential that the air intake screens at the rear of the unit be kept free of lint, hair, and any dirt. **Periodically** check to see that nothing obstructs this flow of air. Unplug the dryer before working on it.

Look at the head or nozzle and you'll see a removable screen that twists off. Remove it and pick off any dirt or hair wedged on the screen. Then clean the intake vents covering the motor.

You can extend the life of the hair dryer's cord if you pull it out of the electrical receptacle by grasping the plug instead of yanking on the cord. Don't twist the cord tightly around the unit when storing it, which can cause the cord to crack. Allow the dryer to cool before you store it with the cord coiled loosely around the unit.

HEAT PUMP

A heat pump unit, located outside your house, is connected to the air-handling unit or furnace inside your house (see the entry on "Furnace," page 47).

At least once a year have the heat pump serviced by a professional. Here are several easy maintenance tasks that you can do to keep your heat pump working most efficiently.

In the fall check the area around the heat pump for overgrown foliage. High bushes or shrubbery planted around the heat pump can shield it from the hot sun in the summer and make the unit more efficient.

While the unit is running, check that no bushes are sucked against the air intake grill, located on the sides of the heat pump. Trim back any bushes or shrubs that disrupt the air flow. Bushes that are too close to the unit will block the air flow through the coils. A free flow of air is essential to transfer heat from inside your house to the outside in the summer and to transfer heat from the outside air to inside your house in the winter.

Leaves and other debris can be sucked into the unit, so look inside the heat pump through the grill and check for a buildup of anything that may block the air. You will have to remove a side panel or lift the cover off the unit to remove these obstacles.

TURN POWER OFF to the heat pump at the main electrical panel before you begin to remove the cover. The cover is held in place by a couple of easily removable screws; check your owner's manual for their exact location. Remove them and lift off the cover.

Clean up the debris, and while you have the cover off, give the coils a wash-down with your garden hose. The compressor and fan motor are weatherproof, but don't direct the hose spray at the control boxes that have electrical lines running into them. Keep your hose spray directed at the coils. When all debris and dirt are cleaned out of the unit, replace the cover.

HEATING DUCT

The large round or rectangular arms that extend out from your furnace are called heating ducts and they carry hot air to the various rooms of a house. **In the fall** when you check your furnace, examine the heating ducts. Use a flashlight (and step ladder, if necessary) to look for air leaks while the furnace is operating. The most likely place where leaks occur is at a joint where the ducts are connected. Begin at the furnace and trace the path of the ducts. Any joints where you feel air escaping should be sealed with heavy gray duct tape.

If the ducts are wrapped in insulation, check to see that the seams in the insulation blankets are tightly sealed with duct tape. Retape any seams that are open or frayed.

Also, check to see that the duct tape or insulation does not cover air intakes, electrical outlets, lighting fixtures, the flue pipe or the chimney.

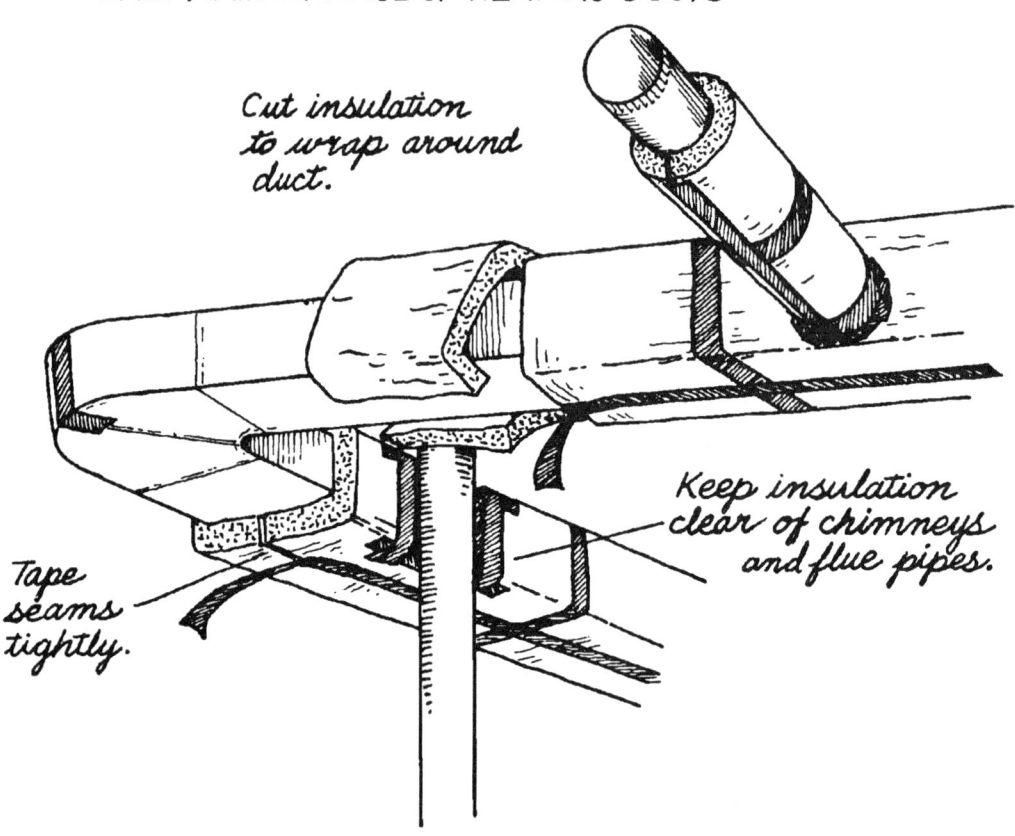

Cut insulation
to wrap around
duct.

Keep insulation
clear of chimneys
and flue pipes.

Tape
seams
tightly.

HUMIDIFIER, Furnace unit

A humidifier is a simple device that evaporates water into the stream of air flowing through the furnace. The evaporation process leaves behind mineral deposits or salt from water conditioners. How long the unit runs and the concentration of solids in your water determine how fast deposits will build up. Depending on the quality of your water supply, a furnace-mounted humidifier may require servicing **once a year or once a month.**

No matter what kind of water you have, clean your furnace-mounted humidifier **at least once a season.** The best time to do this is at the end of the heating season so that the unit will not be filled with corrosive deposits all summer. A week or so before you plan to service the unit, turn off its water supply so that the water in the base has a chance to dry up. The day you service the humidifier, turn off the power to the furnace, and if the humidifier is motor-driven, check that its power is also turned off.

There are several types of furnace-mounted humidifiers but they all work basically the same. Cleaning procedures vary among units so consult your owner's manual for specific instructions on opening your unit, removing the evaporation element, and cleaning it. Here are general guidelines:

To properly service a humidifier, you must take it apart. First, remove the cover, then check that the water is turned off by pushing down on the float mechanism. Remove the evaporation element (a foam-covered drum or disk) when it is encrusted with mineral deposits, and soak it in a sink full of hot water and a mild soap. If that does not remove most of the deposits, soak the element in a half vinegar and half water solution to loosen and dissolve the stubborn deposits. Use a scrub brush to clean the surface.

Some units have a removable water pan liner, which makes cleaning the area easy. First, remove and clean the pan itself. If it's not removable, wipe out the water pan, removing as much waste as possible from the bottom of the unit. Next, clean the float mechanism, which regulates the water level in the unit. Check the owner's manual because some of these units are totally removable, which makes cleaning them a simple job. Be careful not to bend or disturb the setting of the float mechanism.

Clean out the overflow tube if the unit is equipped with one. The overflow tube, which is connected to a standpipe in the bottom of the unit,

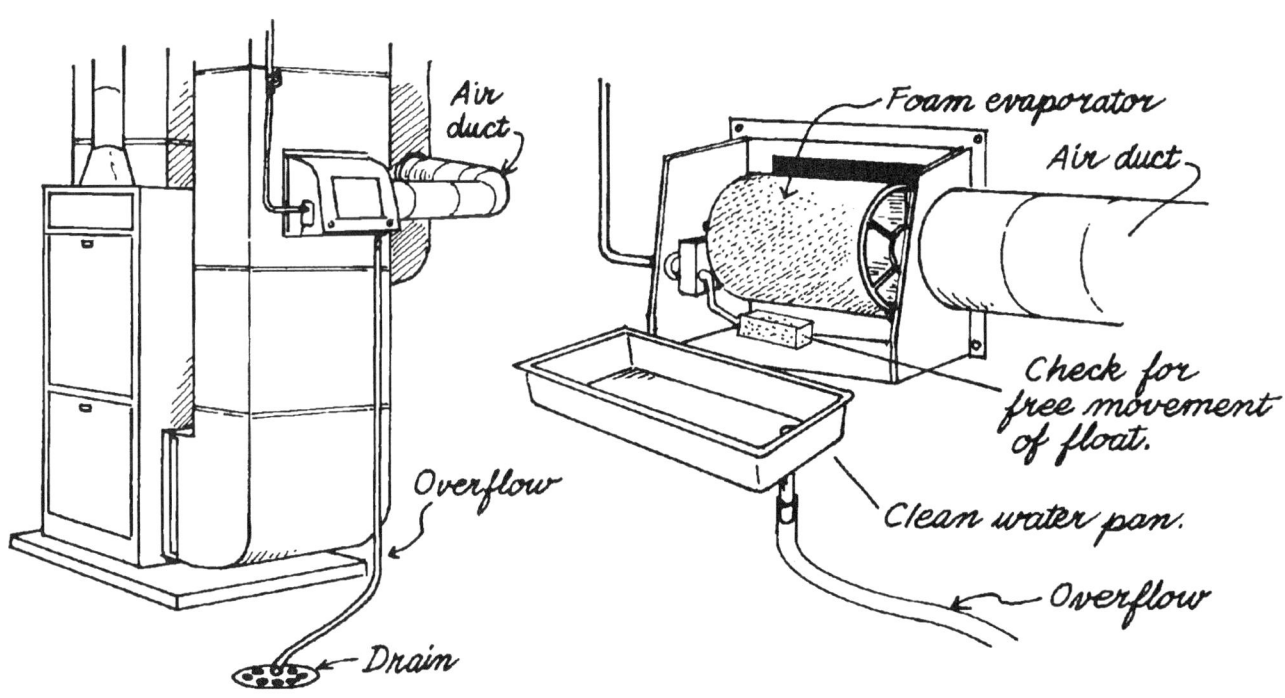

allows water to drain out if the float mechanism sticks. Otherwise the water may run into the furnace and cause it to rust. Clean all deposits from the pipe and from inside the tubing. Test that the overflow tube drains well by pouring some water down it.

When all the parts of the humidifier are clean, reassemble the unit. Put a couple of drops of 20-weight oil on the motor shaft. Unless the owner's manual gives specific instructions on lubricating the plastic parts, don't do it. Most of the parts are loose-fitting and don't require lubrication; in addition, some lubricants can harm the plastic.

Turn the water on to the unit and check that the float mechanism is working. The bottom of the unit should fill with water so that it covers at least the bottom of the foam element. You may have to adjust the float. If the float on your unit is at the end of an arm, bend the arm down slightly to lower the water level and bend it up to raise it. There is usually a water level line on the side of the unit. Consult the owner's manual for specific details.

HUMIDIFIER, Room unit

The quality of the water you put into your room humidifier will determine how much maintenance it requires. Like the furnace-mounted unit, mineral deposits are left behind when the water from the humidifier evaporates into the air.

At least once a season, preferably at the end of the heating season, take the unit apart and give it a good cleaning. Some units are easier to service than others. Check the owner's manual to see if there is a diagram indicating whether the entire motor and evaporator transport mechanisms are removable. If so, cleaning these parts will be a lot easier.

A full humidifier is heavy, so before you plan to service the unit run it for a couple of days to lower the water level. If your humidifier is attached to a water supply by a hose, turn off the water at the faucet.

Unplug the humidifier from the wall and disconnect any hoses. Remove the evaporator element, which is most likely a foam belt or a foam tube stretched over a frame. This mechanism can be lifted straight out of the unit, so it's easy to change.

Soak the element in a mild soap and warm water solution. If it is torn or shows signs of deterioration, purchase a replacement. While the element is soaking, clean the exterior of the unit. Scrub the inside area where the water reservoir pan sits. Remove the pan itself, if possible, for easy cleaning. A solution of half vinegar and half water will loosen and remove most mineral buildup and other dirt.

If your unit is attached to a water supply, carefully clean the float valve assembly. Check that the float arm moves up and down freely and is not rubbing the sides of the unit.

Reassemble the humidifier in the reverse order that you took it apart. Lubricate the motor shaft with a couple of drops of 20-weight oil and check to see that the roller casters, which support the foam element, are running smoothly. They should turn freely. If they bind, apply some petroleum jelly to the joints or use a spray lubricating oil.

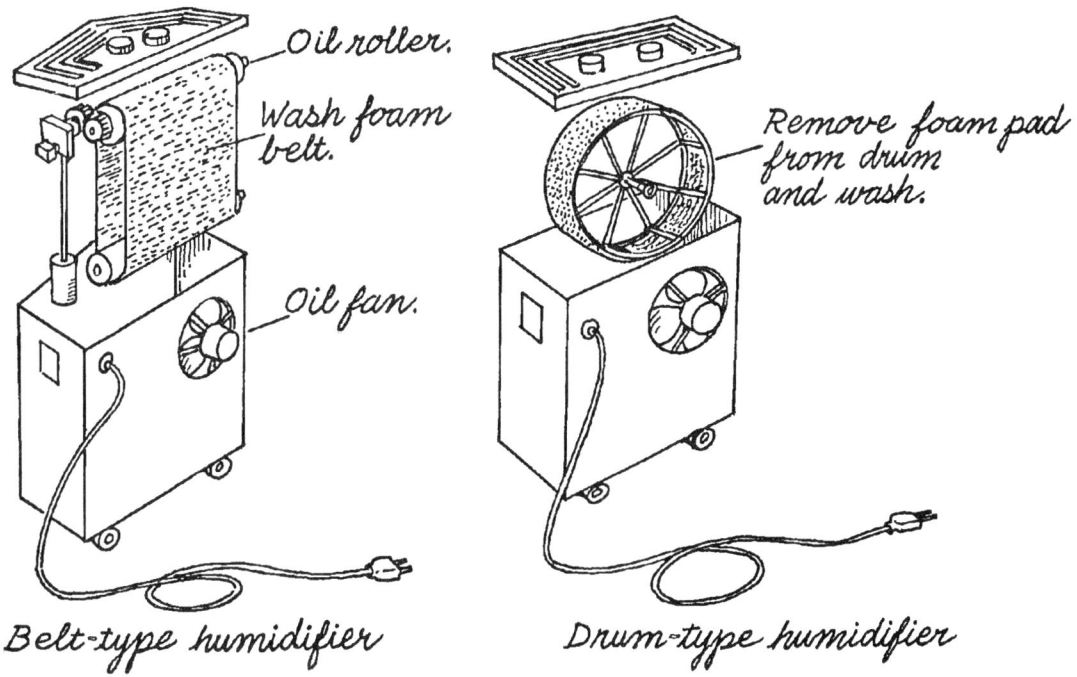

Oil roller.

Wash foam belt.

Oil fan.

Remove foam pad from drum and wash.

Belt-type humidifier

Drum-type humidifier

KNIVES

Ideally, a good knife should be sharpened with its knife steel (a hardened metal rod specially made to sharpen knives) **before every use** so that it requires no maintenance. You can purchase a steel at large hardware stores. If you take a couple of seconds to sharpen your knives before you use them, you won't have to use a dull knife again.

To sharpen a knife, hold the steel in one hand and the knife in the other, with the blade edge facing away from you. Form an "X," with the steel and knife blade crossing near the handles. Work the knife against the sharpening steel at a 20–30 degree angle as you draw it across—first on one side, then on the other side. Repeat this about fifteen times until both sides of the blade are sharp.

Rotary mowers will cut grass with a dull blade but they will work so much better if the blade is sharp. Sharpening a lawn mower blade is easy but you should not sharpen one that has been badly bent. Not only should the blade be sharp, but it should also be in balance or the excess vibration will shorten the mower engine's life.

Remove the blade by loosening the bolt or bolts that hold it to the crankshaft of the engine. Wedge a block of wood between the blade and the side of the lawn mower to keep the blade from turning while you loosen the center bolts.

Replacement blades are not expensive and are available at most hardware stores and home centers. Take the old blade with you so that you can purchase the correct size. Make sure that the number and size of the bolt holes are the same as for the old blade.

If the blade is not bent, you can sharpen it with a coarse file. Put the blade in a vise or clamp it to your bench. Then work the file back and forth several times over the cutting area until the dulled areas begin to show bright new metal. Count your strokes on each side to keep the blade in balance. Don't try to sharpen the blade to a fine point; it will dull quickly. File the blade to its original cutting angle.

When both sides are sharp, balance the blade from its center hole on the shaft of a screwdriver. If one side is heavy, it will dip down, so file away metal from the heavy side. When both sides are even, the blade is in balance. Reinstall the blade and tighten the crankshaft bolt securely.

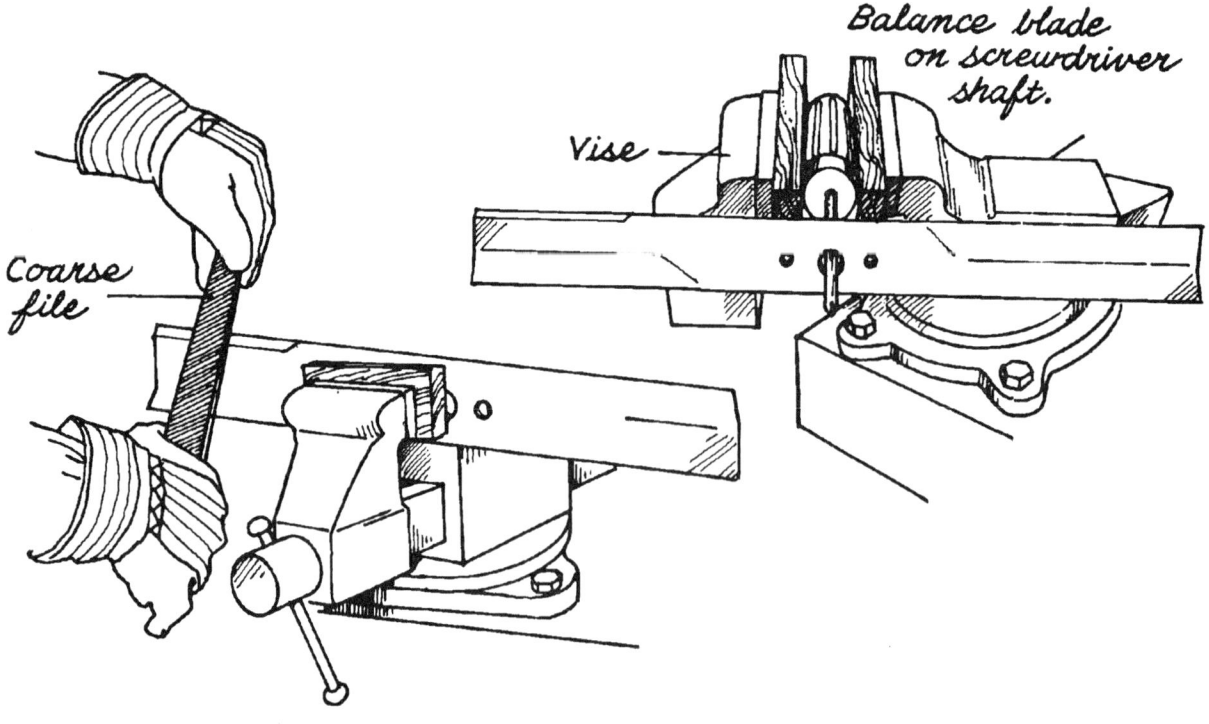

Coarse file

Vise

Balance blade on screwdriver shaft.

LAWN MOWER, Electric

Electric lawn mowers are for the most part maintenance-free. **At least once a year,** preferably at the end of the lawn-cutting season, you should clean the bottom of the mower and sharpen the blade. A dull blade will affect the cutting capability of an electric mower more than that of a gas-powered model because an electric motor is not as powerful.

Unplug the mower before you begin working on it. Turn it over and scrape the grass buildup from under the mower with a stick or putty knife. Then remove the lawn mower blade and sharpen it *(see the entry "Lawn Mower, Blade," page 64).*

It is important for you to use the proper size extension cord with the mower. Long extension cords that are not made of at least 14-gauge wire may harm the electric motor when you cut heavy grass. The cord would be too lightweight to carry the current the motor needs, which in turn would cause the mower and the extension cord to overheat. Several seasons of this abuse and the motor will burn out.

BOTTOM-LINE TIPS: Use a heavy extension cord, keep the blade sharp, and don't let the grass get overgrown so it's too long for the electric mower to cut.

LAWN MOWER, Gas powered

During the mowing season there is not much to maintaining your lawn mower except to keep it full of gas and check the oil a couple of times. But to keep your mower in top shape from season to season you should spend some time **at the end of the mowing season** to assure a quick-starting lawn mower in the spring.

The old oil should be drained out of the engine while it's still hot. Put the mower on a set of sawhorses and remove the oil drain plug. Drain the oil into a wide-mouthed container, then reinstall the drain plug and tighten it. Don't discard the old oil in the garbage; take it to a service station that recycles oil.

While the oil is out of the motor, turn the mower on its side and clean the bottom. Use a stick or screwdriver to scrape off the dried and caked-on grass clippings. If the deposits are hard to remove,

use a scraper or wet the clippings with a hose. Clean the bottom of the mower as well as possible since grass clippings hold moisture and promote rusting during the winter. When the bottom is clean, check the blade. If it's bent, replace it; if it needs sharpening, refer to the entry "Lawn Mower, Blade," page 64. Then turn the mower over and refill the engine with new 30-weight motor oil or with the weight recommended by the manufacturer.

Apply light machine oil to all moving parts. Give special attention to the throttle assembly and cable. Remove the old spark plug and take it to the store to purchase a replacement. Before you install the new plug, turn the mower on end so that the cylinder head of the engine faces up. Pour 1 ounce of 30-weight oil into the spark plug hole and then pull the starting cord slowly to spread the oil inside the engine. Don't pull the cord hard or oil will splash out of the hole. Then replace the spark plug and reattach the spark plug wire.

You can drain the gas out of the tank and run the engine until it stops in order to drain most of the gas out of the carburetor, or you can add gas stabilizer to the fuel tank. Then fill the tank with fresh gas. The stabilizer keeps the gas from gumming up over the winter.

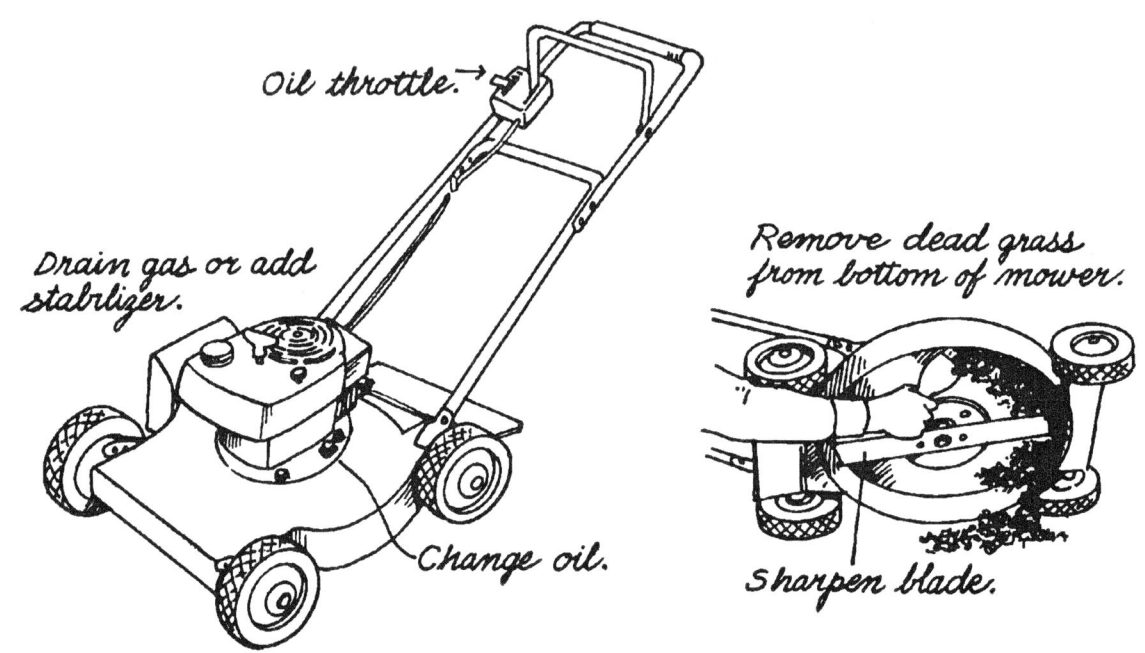

Oil throttle. →

Drain gas or add stabilizer.

Change oil.

Remove dead grass from bottom of mower.

Sharpen blade.

LEAF BLOWER

Gas-powered leaf blowers have a high rpm (revolutions per minute) two-cycle engine that has few moving parts. This type of engine runs trouble-free if you use the proper fuel/oil mixture and service the motor's air filter regularly.

After every five tank fill-ups you should remove the air cleaner element and wash it in soap and water. This filter is usually located at the opposite end of the motor from the spark plug. Some motors have a cover over the filter, so check the owner's manual if you have trouble locating it. Some filters snap into place; others are held in place by a central screw. All are easy to remove.

Wash the filter in hot soapy water, then squeeze

out all excess water. Dry the element by wrapping it in a paper towel and squeezing the water out. When dry, add several drops of lightweight household oil to the element and squeeze it a couple of times to draw the oil into the filter. Then replace it on the motor.

Unless you use the leaf blower every day, replace the spark plug **every other year** or when the motor runs rough or becomes difficult to start. Remove the spark plug wire from the end of the spark plug and use an adjustable wrench to extract the plug by turning it counterclockwise. Take the plug to a hardware store or to the store that sold you the leaf blower and purchase a replacement. Install the new plug, but be careful to hand start it.

The plug should screw easily into the threaded hole in the top of the cylinder head. If you try to force the plug into the hole without proper thread alignment you may cross-thread the plug and damage the threads cut into the soft aluminum cylinder head. Tighten the plug by hand as far as it will go and then use the wrench to tighten it a quarter turn more in the hole. Replace the spark plug wire.

If you store the leaf blower for more than a couple of months, drain all the gas through the fuel cap of the tank and run the engine until it stops. This will assure easy starting when you fill the tank with fresh gas.

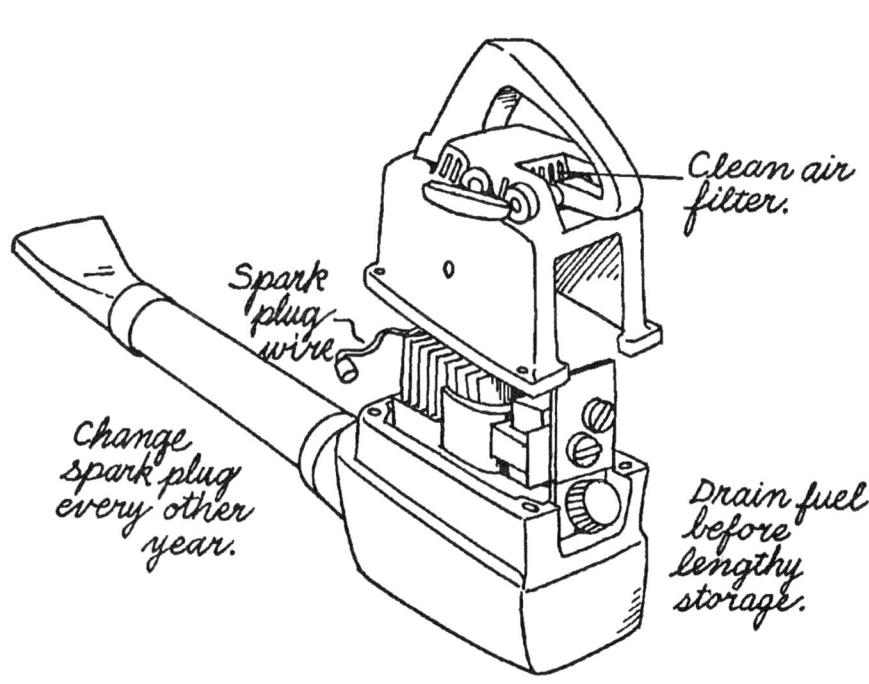

Clean air filter.

Spark plug wire

Change spark plug every other year.

Drain fuel before lengthy storage.

MATTRESS

Extend the life of your mattress by rotating it **periodically** so that the wear is not concentrated in one area. This is especially important when two people of different weights share the same mattress.

Rotating the mattress is a two-person job. With a helper, grasp the hand pulls on the side of the mattress, lift it up to clear the headboard, and then rotate it so that the top of the mattress is at the bottom and vice versa. Some foam and most conventional mattresses may also be flipped or turned over so that each side wears evenly.

PAINT ROLLER

The nap (also called a sleeve) of a paint roller varies according to the condition of the surface being painted. Smooth surfaces should be painted with a short nap roller; textured and rough surfaces require a longer nap. Paint rollers are made of various synthetic materials or natural lamb's wool and are cleaned and maintained in the same way.

When you are finished painting, use the rounded handle part of a paint stirrer to scrape as much excess paint from the roller as possible. You will save a lot of time if you do this before you start cleaning the roller.

Wash the roller in soap and water if you use a latex paint, or soak the roller in mineral spirits if you use an alkyd paint. When the excess paint is removed, use a paintbrush/roller spinner *(see page 69)*, placing the roller in a high-sided bucket to spin dry.

Scrape away as much paint as possible before washing the roller.

PAINTBRUSH, Bristle

A good bristle paintbrush can last a lifetime if it's properly used and cared for. All that is required is a little extra time spent cleaning and storing the brush after its use. Bristle brushes should be used with oil- or alkyd-based paints only. Latex or water-based paints cause the bristles to become limp and the brush does not perform as designed.

If you will be using the brush for several days in a row, it isn't necessary to thoroughly clean the brush after each use. Instead set up a brush-holding can. Pour just enough mineral spirits into the can so that all the bristles are covered. Suspend the brush by its handle in the spirits so the tip of the brush doesn't touch the bottom of the container. Use thin wire or pieces of a coat hanger to make a hook that loops over the side, while the other end of the wire fits through the hole in the top of the brush handle. Loosely cover the can with aluminum foil so the mineral spirits don't evaporate. Another way to do this is to use a large coffee can with a plastic lid and to cut a hole in the lid to hold the brush upright.

After each use, put the brush in the mineral spirits and work most of the paint out of the brush by spreading the bristles while the brush is immersed. Then hang the brush as described in the previous paragraph. The next day, take the brush out of the mineral spirits and shake off the excess with a paintbrush/roller spinner. The spinner is a device with a handle that spins a brush or roller. Its centrifical force will remove most of the mineral spirits. Put the brush in a high-sided bucket or a 5-gallon pail to catch the spray of spirits.

To store the brush for a longer period, first clean it in mineral spirits; then use a wire brush or

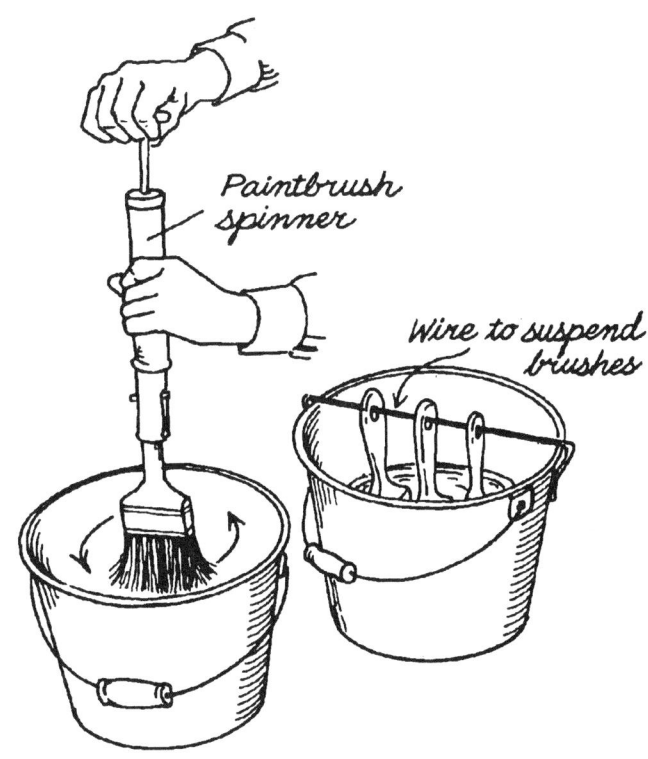

Paintbrush spinner

Wire to suspend brushes

brush comb to remove any caked paint; and then use the spinner to remove most of the spirits. Remove all traces of paint by cleaning the brush again in a water rinse brush cleaner, sold at paint and hardware stores. Work the bristles back and forth in the solution. Be careful not to get any of the solution on your skin since these chemicals may contain strong solvents. Submerge the brush in warm water and mild soap, then rinse completely and spin dry. Shape the bristles of the brush into a compact mass with no loose ends, then wrap the brush in newspaper and secure it with tape or string.

PAINTBRUSH, Nylon, Polyester

Nylon and polyester brushes can be used with oil, alkyd or latex paints. After using the brush with latex paint, rinse it under warm water. Gently separate the bristles to see that all the paint in the heel (where it's attached to the brush handle) is removed. Use a paintbrush spinner to remove the excess water. The spinner works like a child's toy top. The brush handle fits into a holder and as you press the top down, centrifical force spins the brush. If you don't have a spinner, blot the brush with paper towels.

To store the brush for a period of months, clean it thoroughly with a mixture of water and a mild liquid soap. Rinse the brush carefully, then spin dry. Shape the bristles so that there are no stray ends. Wrap newspaper around the bristles to keep them together; then secure the brush loosely with tape or a string.

POWER EXTENSION CORD

How you use and store a heavy-duty power extension cord determines how long it will last. After using the cord, don't pull it out of an electrical outlet with a yank on the cord; grip the cord head firmly and pull it out of the outlet. This handling will prevent the head being severed from the cord.

When it's not in use, keep the cord coiled loosely, not taut (which could cause the rubber covering of the cord to crack). Don't store a power cord on a sharp nail or hook which can pierce and damage the cord.

RADIATOR / BASEBOARD CONVECTOR

To get the most heat out of your hot-water system, the radiators or baseboard convectors must be full of water. Air can get trapped in the upper portions of the radiator and prevent hot water from filling the radiator's chambers.

At least once a year before the heating season begins, bleed (empty slowly) the air from the system. The bleed-valve is located at the top end of the radiator and at one end of the baseboard convector. You may have to remove the radiator cover or open the panel at the end of the baseboard unit to find the valve. Some of these valves have a slotted stem and can be opened with a screwdriver. Many older valves have a square stem and require a "radiator key," a small wrench similar to an old roller skate key. If you don't have one, it can be purchased at a hardware store.

Before you start to bleed air from the system, get a small can or bucket to catch the water runoff from the radiator or baseboard unit. With a

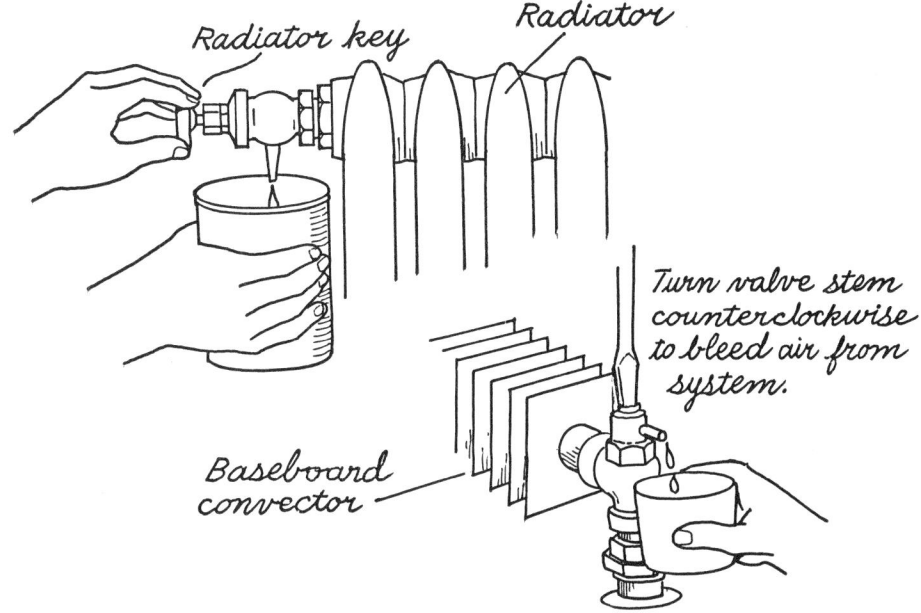

Radiator key

Radiator

Turn valve stem counterclockwise to bleed air from system.

Baseboard convector

"radiator key" or screwdriver, turn the bleed valve stem counterclockwise about a half turn or until you hear air hiss out. You may be surprised how much air is in your radiators if you don't bleed them regularly. There will be less air in a baseboard system.

As soon as the air stops hissing, position the can or bucket to catch the water that will run out of the valve. Allow the water to drain for 10-20 seconds to make sure that all the air is out, then close the valve. Bleed all the radiators or baseboard convectors that have bleeder valves.

During the first week that your heat is on, wait until the boiler is operating and the circulating pump is pushing water throughout the system, then bleed the radiators or baseboard units again. There will be very little air in the system but the pump may move some trapped air to the top of the radiators or high spots in the baseboard system. Be careful when bleeding the units because at this point they contain very hot water.

RANGE, Gas

A gas range is one of the simplest appliances to be maintained in the house. It has few moving parts and when kept clean it will operate trouble-free. The trick to maintaining a gas range is to clean it often before grease or burnt food particles begin to build up.

The part of the stove that you see, namely the top and burner grates, are the least important parts to keep clean as far as proper stove operation is concerned. Food spills that reach into the stove and clog the pilot light burners or settle in the main burners and clog the gas outlet holes will cause the stove to operate erratically.

Most gas ranges have lift-off stove tops or at

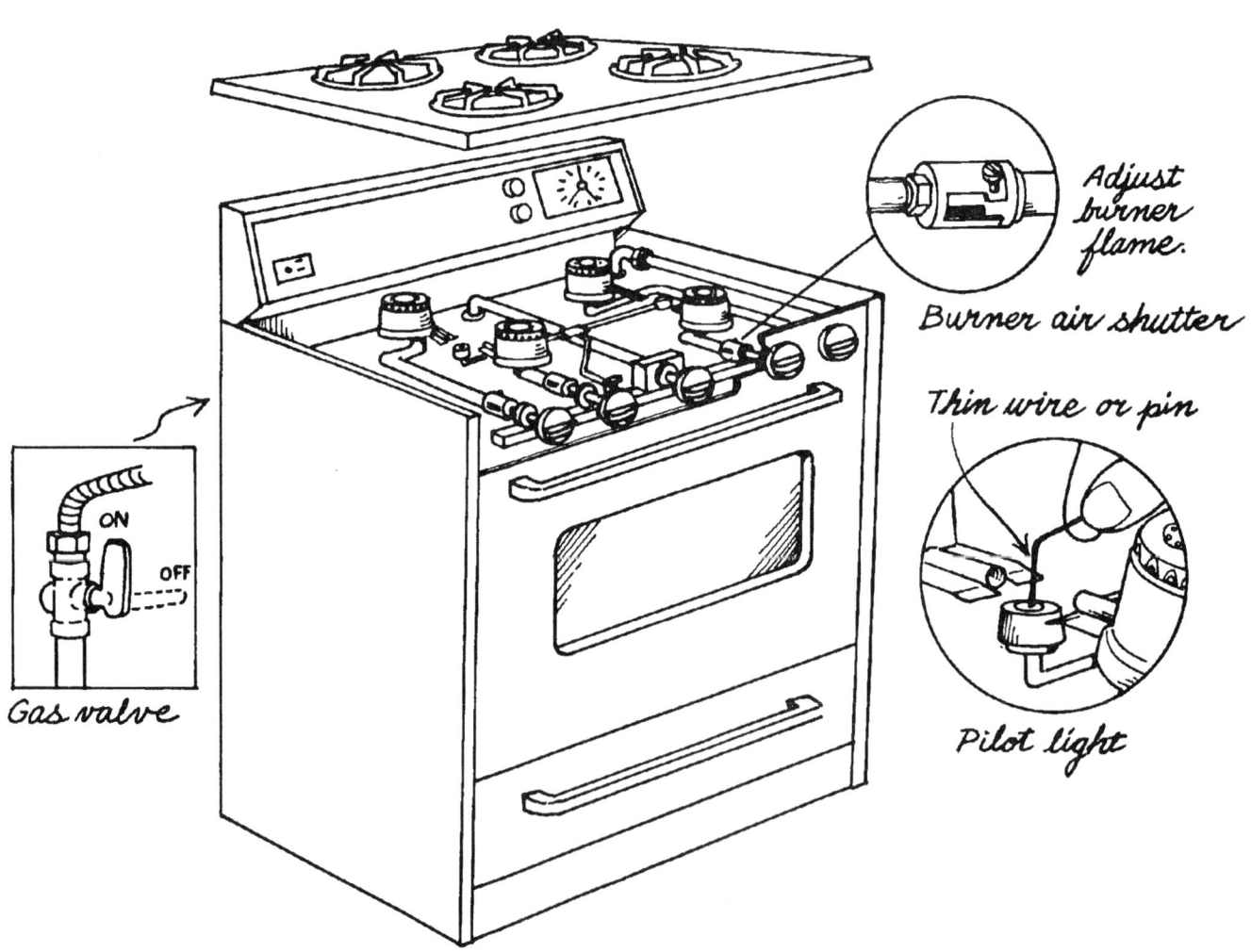

Adjust burner flame.

Burner air shutter

Thin wire or pin

Pilot light

Gas valve

least have lift-up tops. Before you clean a range, turn all the controls to the "off" position and allow the burner grates to cool; then remove the grates from the stove top.

Lift the range top to expose the pilot light and burner assemblies. Check that the pilot lights are lit. If some are not lit, make a note so you can give them a special cleaning. Then turn off the gas valve, which is usually located behind the stove. Turn the handle until it is perpendicular to the gas pipe.

The gas burner assemblies lift out of the stove. Some may have a retaining screw, but they are removable. Take them out, noting where each burner belongs so you can reinstall it properly. Soak the burners in hot soapy water while you clean the other parts of the stove.

Make sure that the pilot light burners are cool before you touch them. Clean away any caked or burnt food buildup with an old toothbrush or other small stiff brush. Use a pin or thin soft wire to clean the pilot gas jet. This small hole is easily clogged with food spills.

Clean the rest of the stove, especially the areas directly under the burners where food spills land. Then thoroughly clean the burner assemblies you left soaking. Remove all food particles from the gas passages located in the outer edge of the burner head. Rinse the units and dry them thoroughly.

Reassemble the stove burners and turn on the gas. Light the pilot light by holding a lit match close to the small gas outlet in the tip of the pilot burner. You may have to wait a little while for the gas to work its way up to the pilot lights. If you have trouble lighting the pilots, turn on one of the main burners for a few seconds to let the air out of the system. Don't keep it on for more than 30 seconds, and turn it off as soon as you smell gas. Wait 5 minutes before you attempt to relight the pilot light in order to allow any accumulation of gas to dissipate. Then light the pilots.

To see how the main burners function, turn them on one at a time. They should ignite right away and burn with an even flame. If the flame is yellow or solid blue, the air/gas mixture is incorrect. Loosen the set screw on the side of the burner air shutter, located at the end of the burner tube. Adjust the air shutter by twisting it slowly to open or close it until the flame burns bright blue with just an occasional yellow tip. Then tighten the shutter set screw and adjust the other burners in the same way.

Replace the stove top and burner grates and your gas range is ready to use again.

RANGE HOOD

A range hood is an important element of a kitchen. It not only provides light to the cooking area, it also removes most unwanted cooking odors and fumes and traps grease and dirt in its filter. To keep the range hood functioning properly and safely, you should clean the grease filter on a regular basis. If greasy dirt is allowed to build up on the filter, it not only will restrict the amount of air the fan can exhaust but can become a fire hazard.

At least once a year, more often depending on how often you cook, remove the filter and clean it. First of all, turn off the power to the range or stove at the electrical panel. Then remove the filter, which is usually located under the range hood directly in front of the blower air intake. Most filters snap out, but some are held in place with clips. These filters are designed to be easy to remove; consult your manual if you can't figure out how to remove the filter from your particular range hood.

Wash the filter in hot soapy water. Use an old toothbrush or pot scrubbing brush to scour between the grill louvers. Dry the filter with paper towels. While the filter is drying, clean the inside of the blower or fan housing. Also clean the round blower assembly (called the "squirrel cage"

because it looks like a small drum that is placed in hamster cages). Clean between the fins or where a buildup of dirt can severely restrict the flow of air through the fan. Reassemble the filter before restoring power.

To clean the exterior and interior of the range hood, wash all surfaces with a damp rag soaked in warm water and soap. If there's a buildup of grease, first wipe down the surface with paper towels, then use a grease-cutting cleaning solution to wash it.

See also entry for "Fan, Exhaust."

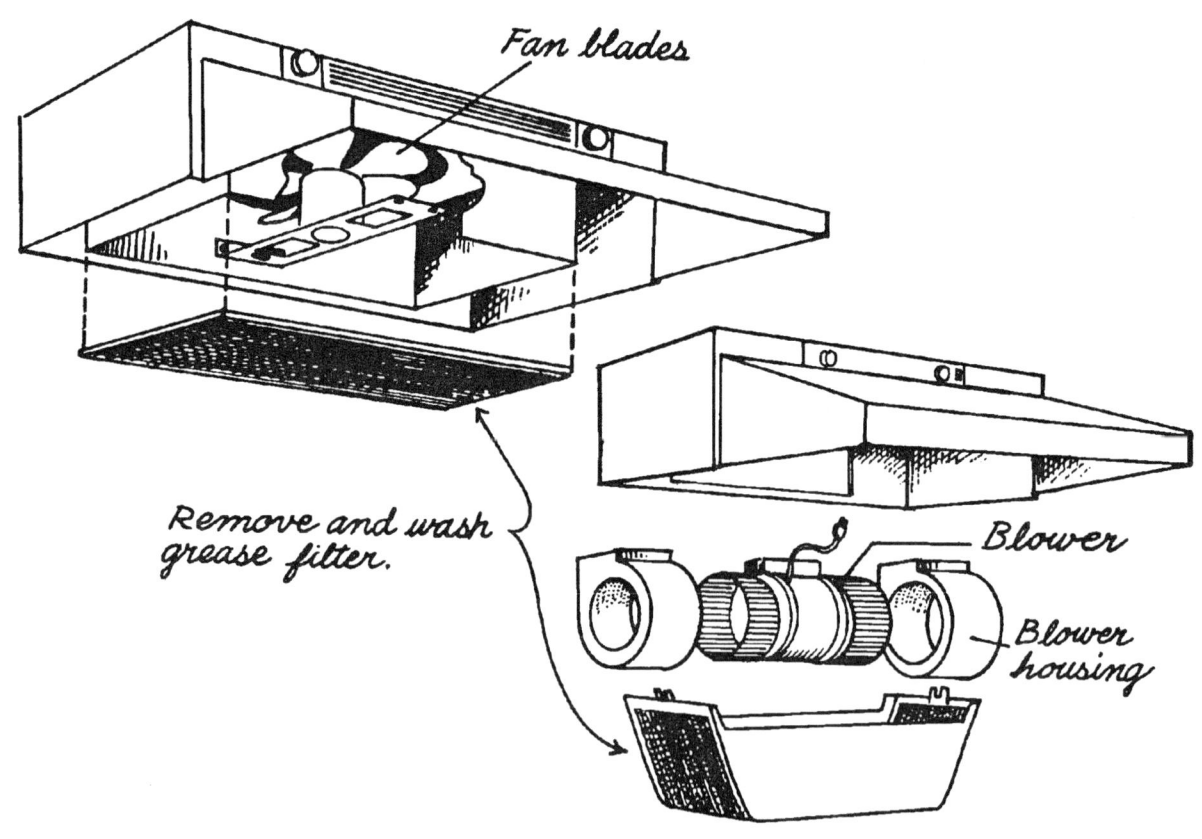

Fan blades

Remove and wash grease filter.

Blower

Blower housing

REFRIGERATOR, Frost-free

Your refrigerator is one of the longest-lasting appliances in your house. It has a sealed compressor motor system that requires no maintenance. However, a refrigerator does consume a huge amount of energy each year and there are several simple maintenance tasks that you can do to assure their efficient operation.

In addition to regular cleaning with warm soapy water, *every few months* clean the condenser coils located on the bottom or back of the unit to remove dust and lint buildup, which can prevent the free flow of air from inside the unit to the air outside. If you keep this area clean, your refrigerator will use less electricity. Use a long-handled brush (like the one designed for removing snow from a car's windshield) or the crevice tool of your vacuum to handle the job.

If your refrigerator has a drain pan at the bottom, clean it regularly or *at least twice a year,* because dirt in this damp area can cause unpleasant odors. If there is a drain, *once a year* fill a meat baster with a warm water and baking soda mixture and force the mixture through the drain to freshen it.

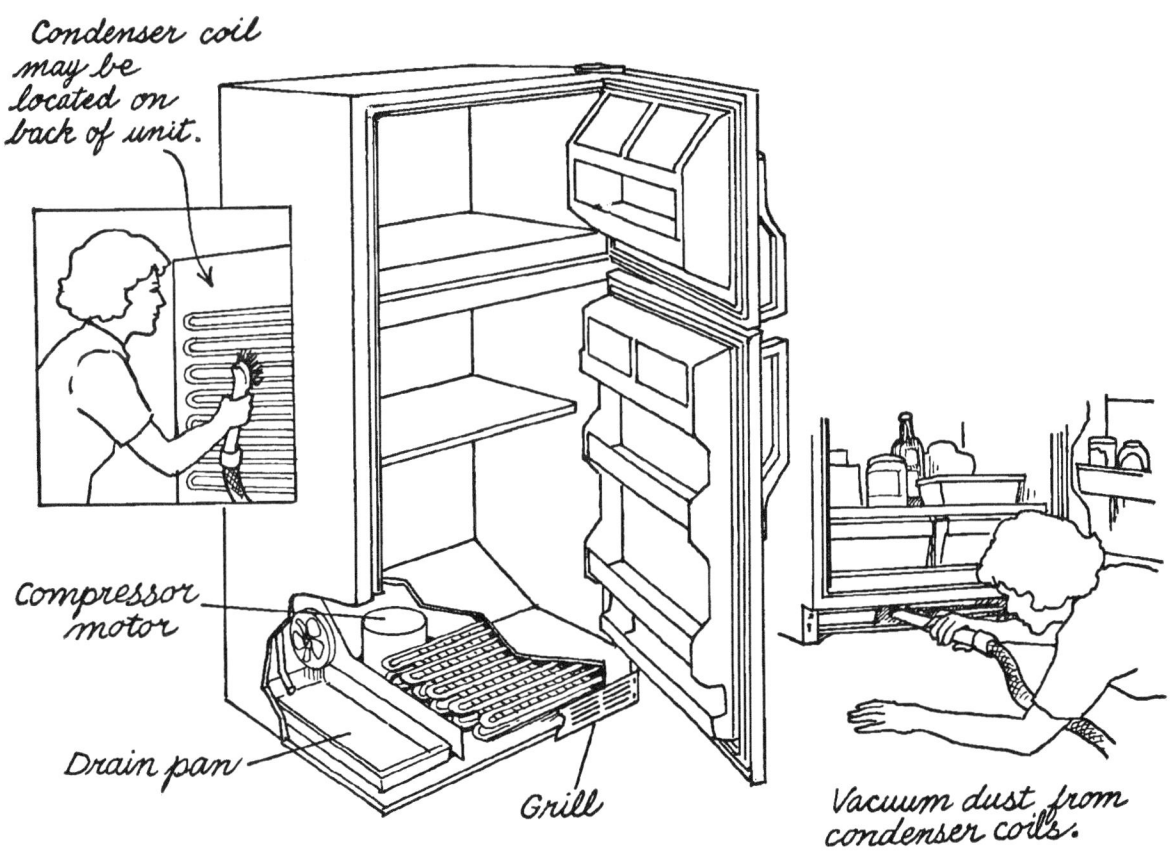

Condenser coil may be located on back of unit.

Compressor motor

Drain pan

Grill

Vacuum dust from condenser coils.

SAW, Circular

Most of today's popular-priced, non-professional power tools, especially circular saws, are designed to be maintenance-free. These tools have double-insulated grounding systems that can be defeated if they are improperly serviced. There are, however, several easy maintenance procedures that you can perform **on a regular basis** that will extend the life of a saw.

First and foremost, always use a sharp saw blade. This is very important when using a consumer-grade saw to cut 2×4 or larger pieces of wood. A dull blade requires more power to cut the same piece of wood than a sharp blade does. A dull-bladed saw has to draw more current and that causes the motor to run hot.

Let your saw do the work; don't force it beyond its capacity. When you are cutting a lot of $1\frac{1}{2}$-inch-thick wood, your saw will heat up. If it is uncomfortable to touch the metal parts, such as the gear case or motor housing, stop operating the saw. Let it run free and gradually cool.

Another cause of overheating is low voltage. A 10 percent drop in line voltage at the tool end of the cord will cause loss of power. Your tool motor has to draw more current to do the same work and this excess will overheat it. Use a heavy-duty, grounded, round jacketed extension cord, with at least 14 AWG (American Wire Gauge) if it's under 50 feet long and 12 AWG if it's longer.

A free flow of cooling air through the saw is essential to prevent overheating. Keep the air passages clear of sawdust buildup by blowing it out of the motor housing after 10 hours of use or after running the saw in a dirty environment. Use an air hose or shop vacuum and direct the air blast into the air passages while the tool is running. Also, blow away any carbon dust that has accumulated around the brushes, which are located at the air intake end of the saw. Be sure to unplug the saw, remove the saw blade, and wear protective eye glasses during this operation.

Dry sawdust will absorb the oil from the bearings, so don't remove sawdust buildup from around them. If you keep removing it, new dry sawdust will draw out more oil. Clean around these areas only when an excessive buildup occurs.

After each project using the saw, clean its housing with a rag dampened in water. Don't use harsh chemicals or solvents like carbon tetrachloride, chlorinated cleaning solvents or ammonia because they will damage the plastic housing. Store your tools for long periods of time out of direct sunlight so that the plastic and rubber parts will wear longer.

Check the brushes for wear after cleaning the saw. Turn the tool on and look into the air slots. Slight sparking in the area where the brushes contact the armature is normal. Long sparks that encircle the armature indicate that the brushes are worn and need replacement. If you suspect the tool has worn brushes, consult the owner's manual.

Many popular priced tools have double-insulated housing and brush systems that should be serviced by the manufacturer. If you decide to service the tool yourself, use only exact replacement parts. The design of the brush system contributes to the double insulation of the tool. Substitution of parts can pose a serious shock hazard.

Heavy-duty tools have accessible brushes that you can service. If either brush is shorter than twice its narrowest width, replace the set.

Like the brushes, a saw's bearings are also subject to wear. Heavy-duty saws have sealed ball and roller bearings that are lubricated for the life of the bearing, but some popular priced tools have sleeve bearings that are impregnated with oil when manufactured. These bearings can also be self-lubricating. Consult your owner's manual since some older tools with sleeve bearings require periodic oiling. These bearings are usually located at the armature end of the tool and are covered by a small felt pad. Several drops of oil applied to the pad are all that is necessary. Be careful not to apply too much oil; it can gum up the inside of the saw.

Circular saws have a gear case that encloses a set of reduction gears that are packed in grease. After heavy use the grease becomes gritty with dirt. With normal homeowner usage this grease doesn't have to be replaced until the tool needs a major overhaul. When it becomes necessary to replace the tool's brushes, return the saw to the manufacturer for a complete servicing.

Remember, when operating your saw, wear safety goggles to protect your eyes from sawdust or an unexpected spray of wood particles.

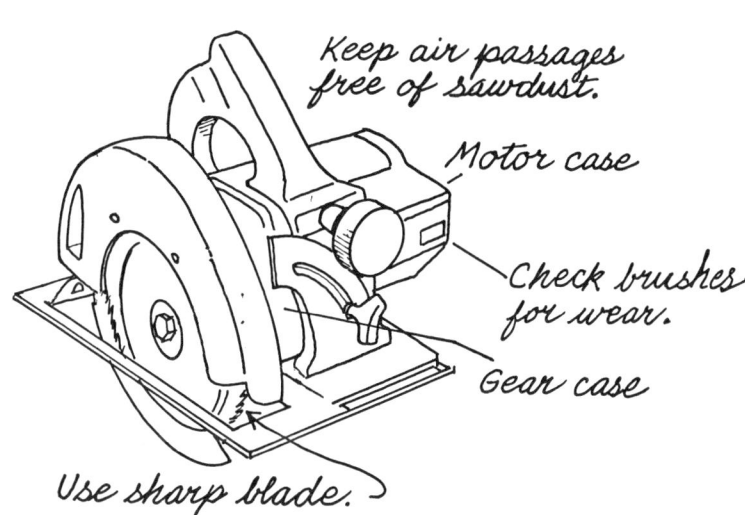

Keep air passages free of sawdust.

Motor case

Check brushes for wear.

Gear case

Use sharp blade.

SAW, Saber

A saber saw (also referred to as a "jigsaw") has an electric motor and brushes that sustain wear, as well as a highly stressed gear case that must change the rotation of the motor to the up-and-down cutting action used by the blade. All saber saws manufactured today have double-insulated motors so that the brush assemblies are not easily accessible. The gear cases of many tools are located inside a plastic case and are difficult to service. These saws are designed to run trouble-free for extended periods and then should be returned to the manufacturer for service.

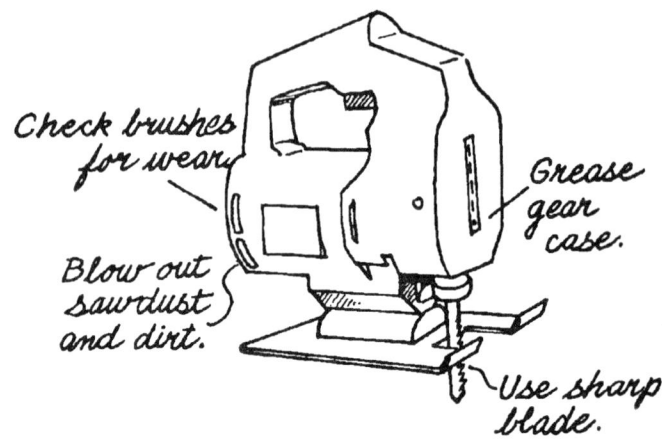

Heavy-duty professional saber saws still have replaceable brush systems. If you have one of these tools and see a lot of sparking around the armature where the brushes make contact, see the entry on servicing a circular saw and brush replacement (page 76).

If the saw has an external metal gear case, then you can service it. Most manufacturers recommend that this be done after *every 100 hours of operation or when the brushes wear down* and the saw requires an overhaul. Consult your owner's manual for specific instructions.

Repacking the gear case is straightforward. Open the case by removing the screw that holds the case together, and expose the gear train. Wipe out the old grease from inside the case with a rag. If your owner's manual explains how to remove the gear train, then take it out and clean the parts; however, if you don't have the manual, leave

the parts in place, remove as much of the old grease as possible, and repack the housing with fresh grease. Use the kind of grease recommended by the manufacturer. Use the same volume of grease as you found in the gear case; too much grease causes excessive drag on the motor. Close up the case and reinstall the housing screws.

Inspect the plug and cord *periodically* for signs of wear. Be suspicious of any plug or cord that feels hot after the tool is used. Broken wires, cracked insulation or high resistance in the plug will make your saber saw run less efficiently and hotter.

Don't store your saber saw for long periods of time in direct sunlight.

SCREENS

The worst enemy of old wire mesh screens is rust. If you leave your screens up all year, eventually they will begin to rust. Newer types are usually made of aluminum wire screen or fiberglass screening fabric. This material won't rust, but fiberglass will eventually be affected by the sun and aluminum will corrode.

You can extend the life of metal wire screens by keeping them painted. The easiest method to paint a screen to prevent it from rusting is to use exterior rust preventive spray paint, which is available in paint and hardware stores. Paint your screen outside on a dropcloth and wear a mask because there's a lot of overspray that you don't want to inhale. Apply several light coats of paint to prevent clogging the screen openings. Use a toothpick to poke out screen holes that catch the paint.

Fabric screening used in most doors and windows today is softer to the touch and not as brittle as the older wire mesh screening that dries and cracks. To extend the life of your screen, it's important to keep it clean. Airborne pollutants will corrode aluminum and attack fiberglass, shortening their life. ***Whenever dust and dirt accumulate,*** clean your screen with a garden hose and a bucket of soapy water. Rinse with clean water, then towel dry the frame and screen.

Newer screen doors and windows have screen panels that are fastened into aluminum frames. Whether they sag, have large holes, or are pushed loose from the frame, they are easy to fix. Remove the thin rubber gasket (called "spline") that holds the screening in the frame. It's usually gray and runs around the screen's perimeter. Find one end and gently pull it out from its groove with a pliers. Lift the screening out.

If the spline is supple, not brittle, it can be

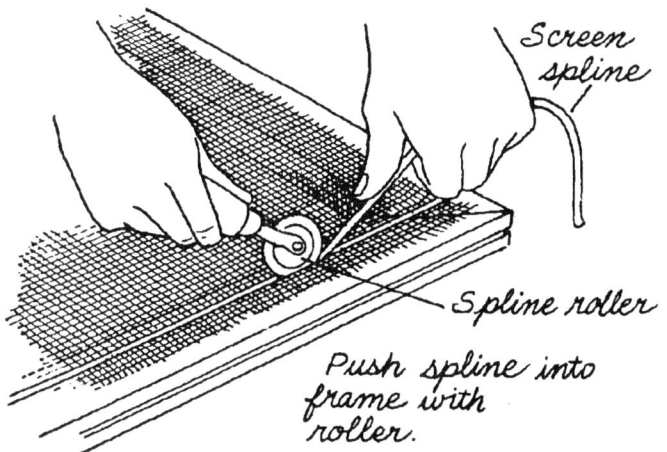

Screen spline

Spline roller

Push spline into frame with roller.

reused; otherwise buy a package of screen spline. You'll also need a screen spline roller which looks like a pizza cutter. This inexpensive tool is a great help when you have to force the spline and screen back into the groove in the frame.

Installing the screening is easy. You'll find replacement screening fabric at hardware stores and home centers. Place the frame on a flat surface with the groove up, then position the screen fabric over the frame. Starting at one corner, force the rubber spline into the groove with the spline roller or use the blade of a large screwdriver. Work around the frame, pushing the spline into the frame. When you get back to the starting corner, cut off the spline. Trim away any excess screening with a utility knife.

If the screening has small tears or holes, patch them with screen patch sold in hardware stores. The patch is a 2-inch square of screening that you place over the tear and weave into the surrounding screen holes. Just tuck the four open sides into the mesh to secure the patch.

SENSOR SECURITY SYSTEM

Large elaborate electronic security systems are, for the most part, self-testing and maintenance-free. Operational problems should be fixed by a professional. However, there are a few things that you can do to keep a wireless system operating reliably. These systems may be self-installed and they have become very popular in the last ten years.

If you have a wireless system, you should check the batteries regularly and replace them *every year.* The main unit has batteries and each sender unit is also equipped with a battery. Alkaline batteries have a long life, but they will run down at different times in the sender and main units, so you are better off replacing all the batteries at one time once a year (or sooner if the manufacturer requires it).

When you are changing the batteries, check to see that the sending unit and sensors are securely mounted. Check that the sensor mounting screws are tight, especially those installed over doors. If the screws work loose, the sensor may shift position and stop operating, or give false readings. Check the wire connections at both the sensor and sender ends. All screw terminals should be tight and the wires secure.

All security systems have a system check mode; be sure to run it periodically to make certain that the system is operating.

SEWING MACHINE

If you look inside a sewing machine, you will find many small moving parts that must all work in perfect synchronization. Because of this, the machine requires lubrication in order to keep everything moving freely. Consult your owner's manual for information about oiling the parts. If you have an older machine and have misplaced the manual, purchase a small can of sewing machine oil sold at sewing centers and hardware stores and follow these general suggestions:

The most important thing to remember when oiling a sewing machine is that a tiny drop of oil is all that's necessary. Over-oiling will not help the machine, and the excess oil will attract and hold dust and dirt, causing excessive wear to the small parts. Oil often, but sparingly.

Place a few drops of oil in the bearings, which are located anyplace that a shaft runs through another part of the machine housing, and at all joints where two parts are attached. Also apply oil sparingly on any part that slides over another machine part.

Open the sewing machine's door or cover to expose the bobbin, which is located in the base of the machine. Remove the bobbin and then run the machine slowly so that you can see which parts require oil.

Also clean and lightly lubricate the exterior metal

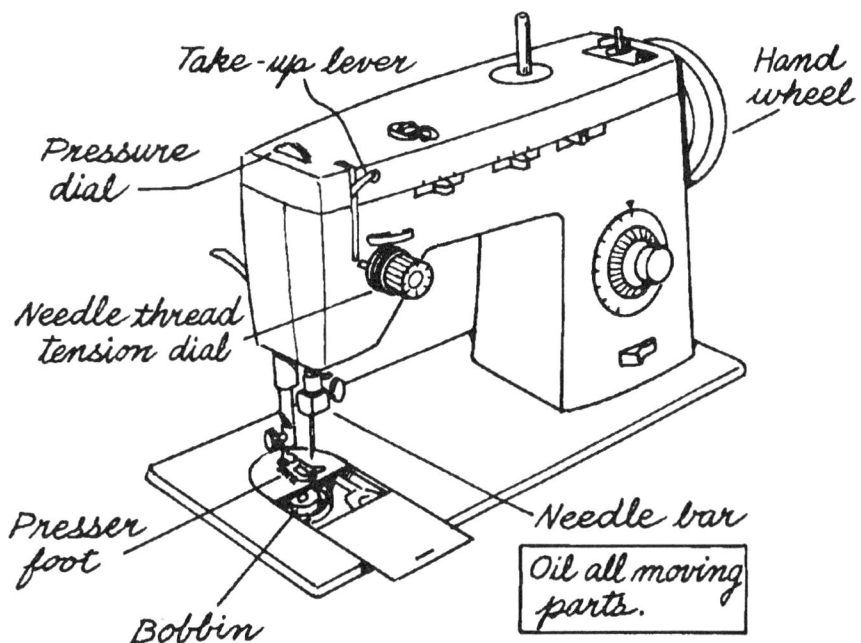

Take-up lever

Hand wheel

Pressure dial

Needle thread tension dial

Presser foot

Bobbin

Needle bar

Oil all moving parts.

parts of your sewing machine that are exposed to hands, fabric, and thread. Squirt a little oil on a rag or paper towel; clean the parts located in the hook area, at the needle bar, and take-up lever and bobbin. Keep these areas lint-free and lightly oiled.

A machine that is used frequently should receive an **annual tune-up** by an approved dealer or service technician.

SHAVER, Corded

Electric shavers that plug into a wall receptacle have powerful little motors that run trouble-free for years, but the cutter assemblies require some attention if you want to get the best performance.

All types (flat, curved, and rotary) of shavers should have their cutter heads cleaned **after each** **use.** To clean, open the head and remove any hair with a gentle tap against the palm of your hand. Most manufacturers supply a small stiff brush to clean the head assembly.

Regular cleaning prevents the motor from being overloaded by the excess friction caused by the hair

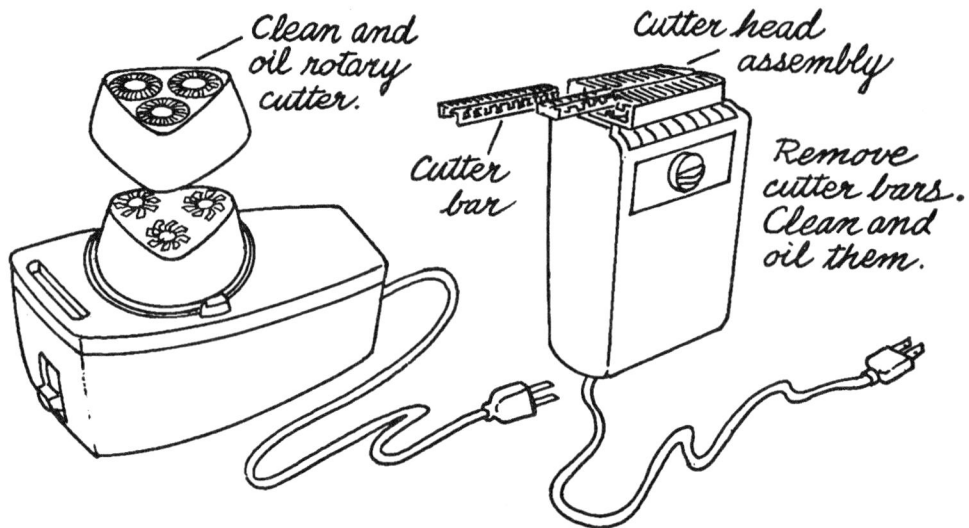

Clean and oil rotary cutter.

Cutter head assembly

Cutter bar

Remove cutter bars. Clean and oil them.

that gets packed into the cutter head assembly when it's not cleaned. **Once a month** unplug the razor, clean out the head, and remove the head assembly. Rinse the head assembly under hot water and dry it thoroughly. Apply a drop of light all-purpose oil to the cutters and reassemble the shaver.

SHAVER, Cordless

A cordless electric shaver runs on batteries and has less power than those that plug into an electrical outlet. Keeping the cutter head clean will extend the number of shaves you can expect from one charging and lengthen the life of the batteries.

Maintenance of the cutter head of a rechargeable shaver is exactly the same as its corded counterpart. Recharge the shaver **when** *the motor begins to run slow.* Occasionally run the batteries completely down so that the motor stops before you fully recharge the shaver.

When the shaver wears out, don't throw it into the garbage; it will end up in a landfill where NiCad batteries are a major source of heavy metal pollution. Instead, call your local recycling center and ask where to dispose of the shaver.

SHOVEL

After each use, clean the dirt from a garden shovel with a hose and let it air dry in the sun. A shovel with a sharp edge is easier to dig with. It will also make cutting small roots quite easy.

Sharpen a shovel with a single-cut file. This type of file cuts in only one direction. Put the shovel in a vise and hold the file perpendicular to the blade; then work the file across the blade as if you were sharpening a knife.

When signs of splinters appear on the shovel's handle, give the wood a good sanding with a sheet of medium-grit sandpaper folded in half lengthwise. Work the sandpaper up and down and around the handle until all surfaces are smooth. Polish the wood with a thin coat of tung oil.

SHOWER HEAD

The aerator or holes in a shower head can be clogged with mineral deposits from the water. To keep a shower head running freely and efficiently, **periodically** unclog the holes. Use a straight pin to unplug the openings or remove the aerator screen and clean it. Soak this screen in a mixture of half water and half white vinegar for 10 minutes; then rinse in clear water and reinstall.

SMOKE DETECTOR

A smoke detector is a safety device that you hope you will never hear. But since these devices are silent until they announce a potentially life-threatening situation, proper maintenance is a must.

All units have a tester button and some have a light-sensitive area that allows you to check the unit when you shine a flashlight on it. Some units beep when the battery gets low. Check your smoke detectors **monthly** by pressing the test button, which will sound the alarm. Don't rely on the unit to tell you when it is malfunctioning.

A regular scheduled battery check and replacement is the only way to assure faithful operation. A handy time to check the batteries in smoke detectors is **twice a year** when you change your clocks to "Spring ahead" and "Fall back." At one of these times, replace the battery even if it still

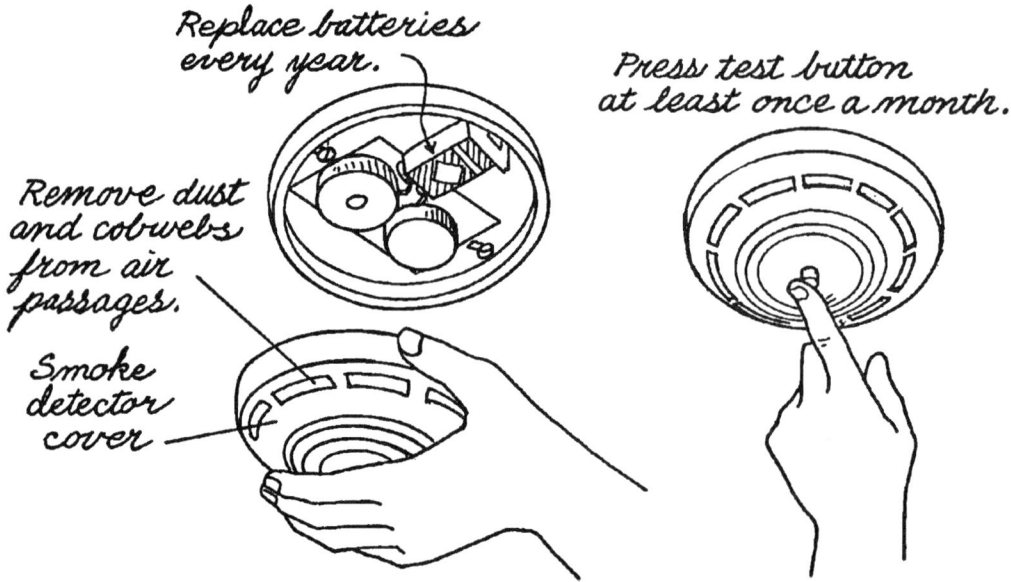

Replace batteries every year.

Remove dust and cobwebs from air passages.

Smoke detector cover

Press test button at least once a month.

has some life left in it. Use the still good battery from the smoke detector in a radio or some other appliance.

Keep the smoke detector working efficiently by clearing the smoke entry holes of dust or cobwebs. Use the crevice tool of a vacuum, or a small paintbrush, to dust out the air passages in the cover.

STORM DOOR WINDOW

A combination aluminum storm and screen door is built to withstand the weather and it's made durable for continued use. To keep it working longer and better, make a habit of oiling its hinges **twice a year** with a silicone spray or a light all-purpose oil.

After several seasons of changing the screen panel to the storm window panel, the threads in the door that hold the panels begin to wear down. The retaining clips that screw into the tracks become difficult to tighten or fall out completely.

An easy solution to this common problem is to replace the worn clips with a 3/4-inch-long #8 panhead sheet metal screw and a large washer. Drill a new 1/16-inch-diameter hole into the door frame next to the bad clip. Use a pair of pliers to bend the washer in the center just a little so that it forms a wide V. This causes the washer to push against the screen or storm sash when the sheet metal screw is tightened. Then insert the screw

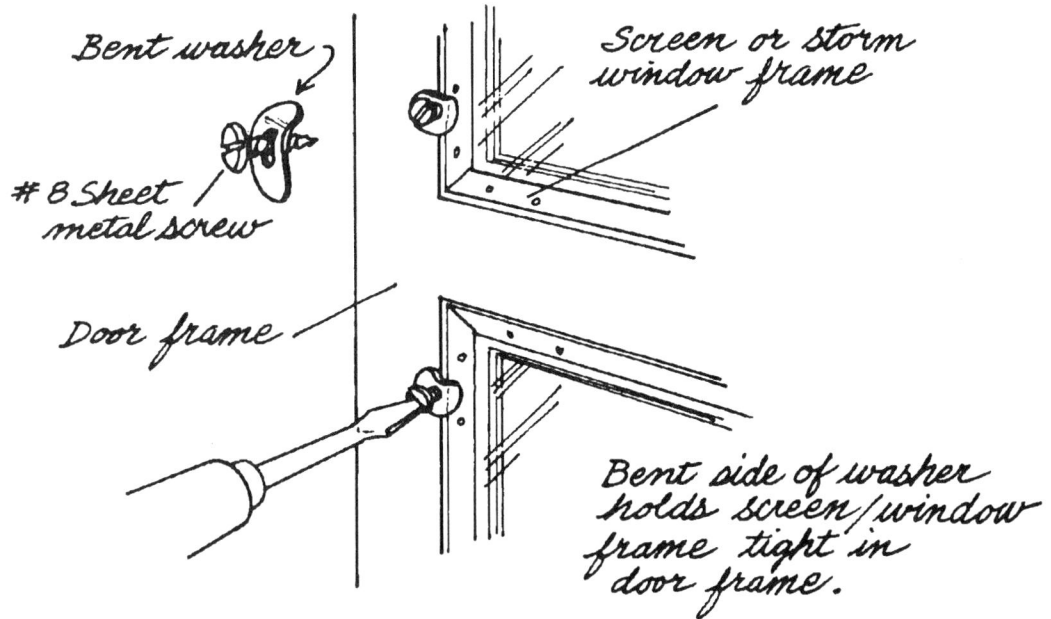

Bent washer

#8 Sheet metal screw

Door frame

Screen or storm window frame

Bent side of washer holds screen/window frame tight in door frame.

through the washer, with the bent part of the washer facing the door frame. Tighten the screw to pull the washer tight against the frame. The bent part of the washer will push against the screen or window panel and hold it in place. Do this in several areas around the perimeter of the panel to hold it firmly in its frame.

STOVE PIPE, Chimney connector

Chimney connectors, located inside the house, get so hot that at times the protective coating or paint burns off the pipe, exposing bare metal. To prevent rust from forming on an unpainted stove pipe (which is usually blue in color), here's what to do. Give the stove pipe a dry wipe-down, followed by a light application of stove polish **at least once a year,** preferably at the end of the heating season. An enameled stove pipe should be wiped down with a damp rag and then dried. *(See the entry on "Wood Stove," page 106, about treating an enameled surface.)*

Double- or triple-walled pipe that is not painted at the factory—but has been painted to match your stove—will eventually begin to discolor and peel, especially in the area close to the stove where the temperatures are extremely hot. Except for burning the stove at a much lower temperature, there is no way to prevent this from happening. Painting the stove pipe is not difficult.

High-temperature silicone-based spray paint in a color that matches the stove is available from most stove suppliers or at some large paint stores. Two cans will supply two coats of paint on a typical 5-foot-high pipe. Have the paint store put the cans of spray paint on a paint shaker to mix completely the pigments with the silicone resins. High-temperature paint gives off hazardous fumes, so do your painting outside or provide good ventilation. ALWAYS WEAR A RESPIRATOR.

Use a wire brush to remove the old flaking paint; sand the rough edges smooth. As you apply spray paint, stop often to shake the can vigorously to keep the paint mixed. Let the first coat of paint dry for 45 minutes before recoating.

The first few times you use the stove in the fall you may notice some smoking from the pipe but it will stop after the pipe heats up.

Use wire brush to remove loose and flaking paint on stove pipe.

STRING TRIMMER

A string trimmer makes short work of cutting and trimming grass that grows next to trees, fences, and buildings. It's a lawn tool that's powered either by a gas or electric motor which turns a small drum at the end of a long shaft. Inside the drum is a spool of monofilament line. A short piece of this line is allowed to protrude from the spool and whips around so fast that it can actually cut grass and weeds.

Gas powered string trimmers are the most popular today, but both gas- and electric-powered units use the same type of spool and line assembly. If you have an electric unit, skip the motor maintenance section below and follow the **yearly** shaft and spool lubrication.

Gas-powered string trimmers have simple high-speed 2-cycle motors that run trouble-free and are easy to start if you give them a minimum of care. Since a string trimmer is used in dirty, dusty conditions, its air cleaner is the system's first defense. Proper lubrication of the flexible shaft and cutting string replacement are the other two areas that require regular maintenance.

After each use or during cutting (after you have turned off the motor), remove any long grass or other debris lodged around the trimmer head. Eventually you will have to install a new spool of cutting line. Follow the manufacturer's directions exactly. This part of the trimmer rotates at high speed and can cause serious injury if it's not installed according to the manufacturer's directions. Do not reuse any cracked or bent parts, and use only replacement parts and cutting string spools designed for your trimmer.

After 5 hours of operation or five tanks of fuel, clean the air filter, which is usually located near the gas tank. Some trimmers have snap-off filters; others have filters that are held in place with screws or hex nuts. Remove the fasteners or pull the filter off the motor. Wash it in soap and water. Squeeze out the water and let the filter dry before putting it back in place.

After about 10 hours of operation, lubricate the flexible drive shaft located inside the long metal tube connecting the motor and the cutter head assembly. Follow the specific directions given by the manufacturer of your particular trimmer. Purchase a tube of shaft lubricant from the store where you purchased the trimmer.

To apply the lubricant, you have to loosen the retaining screws that hold the tube in the motor assembly. Place some newspapers on a flat surface where you set the flexible shaft. Since the shaft is covered with grease, it should be placed on a clean surface where it won't pick up dirt or debris. Pull the tube out of the motor assembly, then pull the flexible shaft from the tube and lay it on the newspapers.

Wipe the old grease off the shaft with a rag, being careful not to cut your hand on any sharp wire barbs that may stick out of the shaft where it's worn. If there are any loose wires, replace the shaft. Otherwise, grease and replace it in the tube, then reinstall the tube on the front of the motor assembly. Check to see that the end of the flexible shaft is fully seated in the drive socket of the motor. Then tighten the retaining screws.

At the end of the lawn trimming season drain the gas tank and carburetor so that they are empty. Start the motor with the choke on full and run the motor until it stops. Then store your trimmer in a clean, dry place.

Drain gas for storage.

Motor assembly

Lubricate flexible drive shaft every 4 years.

Replace string spool if empty or cracked.

SUMP PUMP

A sump pump is used to remove water from a basement or crawl space. It usually is placed in a pit, located in the basement floor or under the house, called a sump. The pump is designed to start pumping when the sump begins to fill with water. Since a sump pump is very reliable and out of sight, it tends to be neglected until there is a problem. Don't let 6 inches of water in your basement be the reminder to take a look at your pump. Most sump pump disasters are easy to avoid. Here's how:

To keep your sump pump in good working order, inspect it regularly. A quick visual check is all that's necessary. Keep a flashlight handy for you to see into the pump pit if it's in a dark corner of the basement.

Periodically, and especially after a heavy rain, make sure that the bottom of the pit is clean and that there's no buildup of sand, dirt, or debris that can clog the pump or jam the motor and burn it out.

Check that the float is free to move up and down

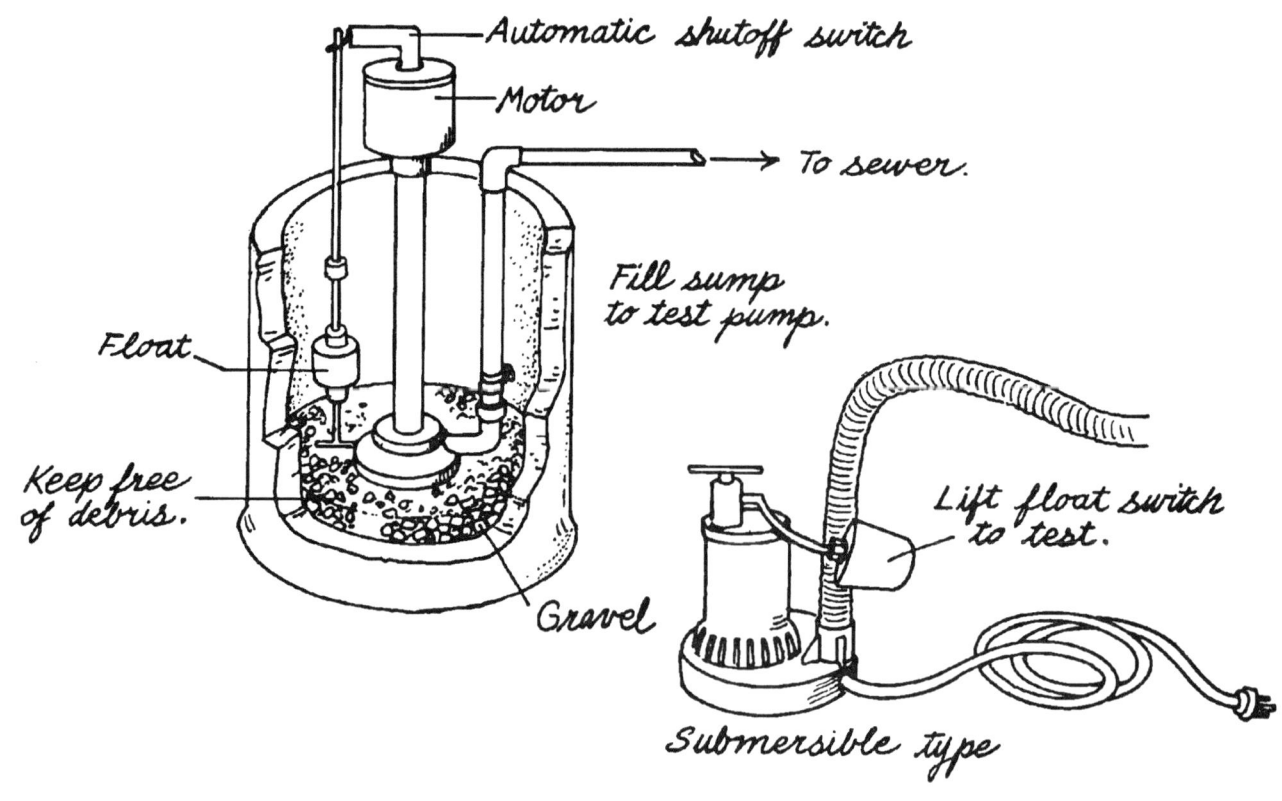

Automatic shutoff switch

Motor

To sewer.

Fill sump to test pump.

Float

Keep free of debris.

Gravel

Lift float switch to test.

Submersible type

and will activate the pump when lifted. Submersible sump pumps have a switch located at the end of a cord. The float switch rises with the water level until it finally tips up, closing the switch. To test this switch, lift the float and the pump should start as soon as the float is turned up. Non-submersible pumps have float switches that run up and down a rod. To test the switches, raise the float up the rod until the pump starts. Remove debris or other objects that prevent the free movement of the pump float switch.

At least once a year, preferably in the spring before the rainy season, check the working of the pump. If you have observed that the pump works at some other time, then skip the test. Use a garden hose to fill the sump with water and watch to see that the pump starts. It should be able to empty the sump much faster than a garden hose can fill the sump.

If the pump doesn't empty the sump pit, check the circuit breaker at the main panel. If it is open or the fuse is blown, replace them. Then test the pump again. If the pump doesn't work properly again, have it serviced, because a sump pump must be reliable or you could face a flooded basement.

TAPE PLAYER / RECORDER, Portable cassette

Cassette players operate trouble-free if they are given occasional maintenance. The magnetic recording tape inside the cassette cartridge rubs against the record/playback head of the recorder whenever it's in operation. Some of the tape's magnetic coating rubs off onto the head and other moving parts of the tape transport mechanism, and this buildup eventually worsens the performance of the recorder. Cleaning the record/ playback head and the tape transport mechanism will keep your recorder working longer and performing better.

After every 20 to 30 hours of playing time, clean the record/playback head and all moving parts in the cassette compartment. Use a head-cleaning solution sold at record or electronic stores; denatured alcohol also works. You'll also need some cotton-tipped swabs.

Turn the recorder off or remove the batteries so the unit will not play when you depress the play or forward buttons. Remove the cassette, if there is one, in the recorder. Then depress and lock the "forward" button, which moves the record/ playback head out from the side of the cassette compartment.

Dampen a cotton swab with denatured alcohol or the commercial cleaner recommended in the recorder owner's manual. Gently wipe the play/ record head (or heads, if they are separate) with the swab. Remove as much brown oxide as possible, but don't flood the head or area around it with liquid.

Next, clean the capstan and pinch rollers, which are located on the right side of the tape recorder head. The magnetic tape is squeezed between the metal capstan post and the small rubber roller, and

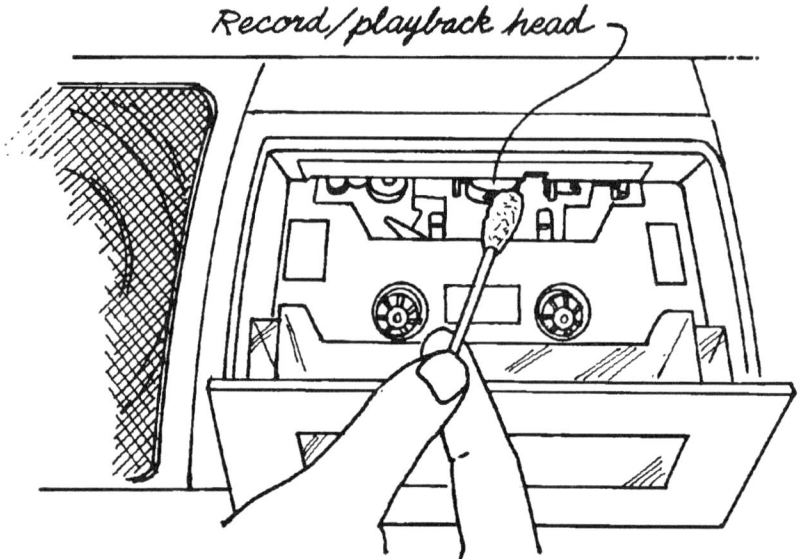

Record/playback head

Clean tape recorder head
with denatured alcohol.

pulled past the head. Remove any brown oxide buildup with the damp swab. Also clean the roller or post to the left of the head. Release the "forward" button and set the recorder aside with the cassette door open to allow all the cleaning fluid to evaporate.

If a cassette has a slack tape, don't touch it. Instead, take up the excess slack in the tape by inserting the eraser end of a lead pencil into the transport hole on the right side of the cassette. Then turn the spool clockwise to rewind the tape.

If it's a short loop, use your little finger to rewind the tape. Remember: The tape moves from right to left, so to rewind the tape on the right spool, turn the spool clockwise; to rewind the tape on the left spool, turn the spool counterclockwise.

Store a portable cassette recorder in dry conditions; don't keep it in a dusty or hot area like a car glove compartment. Remove the batteries if you won't be using the recorder for longer than a month.

90

TELEPHONE ANSWERING MACHINE

A telephone answering machine has a cassette recorder inside, and this interior compartment is the only area that requires maintenance. *(See the prior entry on maintenance tips for a Tape Player / Recorder, which are also applicable for this machine.)*

To extend the longevity of an answering machine, place the unit in an area free from dust, moisture, high temperature, and vibration. Avoid bringing metal or magnetic objects (which can magnetize the heads) near the machine. The best location is an area away from heating appliances and electrically noisy equipment such as fluorescent lamps, motors or televisions because these devices can interfere with the machine's performance.

If the unit has a remote beeper that allows you to listen to the recorded calls over the telephone, replace its batteries *once a year.* If the beeper unit is not going to be used for a long period of time, remove the batteries to avoid battery leakage.

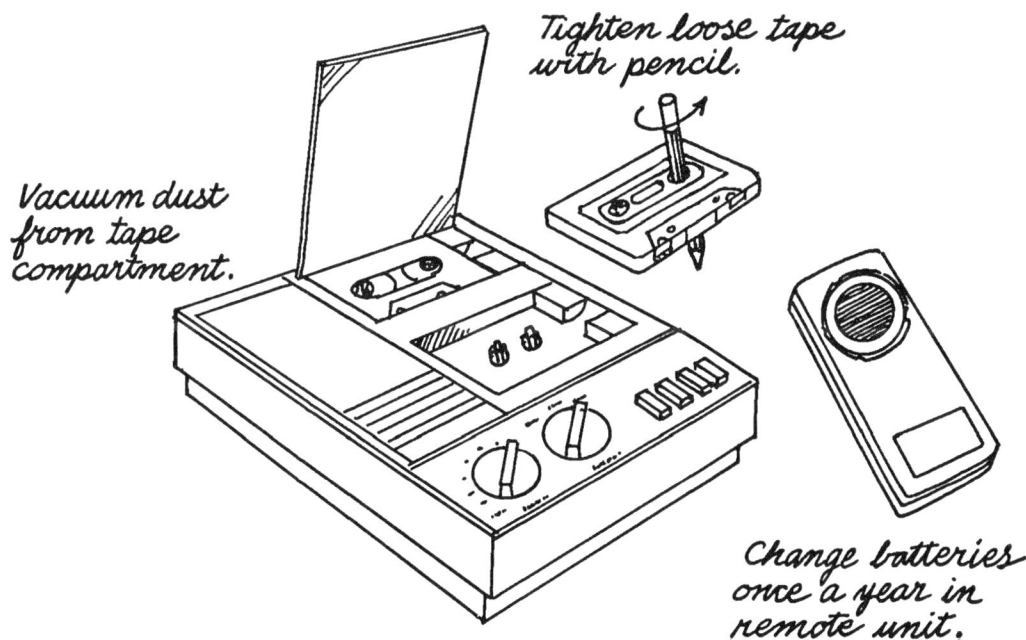

Vacuum dust from tape compartment.

Tighten loose tape with pencil.

Change batteries once a year in remote unit.

THERMOSTAT, Electronic

Electronic thermostates come in two types: Clock or setback thermostats may contain a mercury-switch-type thermostat, or if the unit has a digital temperature readout it probably contains a solid state (all electronic) thermostat switch. In either case the unit should be cleaned out **at the beginning of the heating season,** just like a standard manual unit *(see entry below).*

If the unit contains a battery, it should be replaced. This 9-volt transistor radio battery is usually located in its own compartment. Open the battery door and remove the battery, which has a snap-off type connector. Install the new battery by pushing the snaps over the terminals. This connector can only be put on one way in order to assure that proper polarity is maintained.

THERMOSTAT, Manual

Thermostats are extremely simple devices with few moving parts but dust can build up inside these units and cause them to give false readings or to malfunction. **At least once a year,** preferably before the heating season, open the cover of your thermostat and remove any accumulation of dust.

Most covers just snap off and expose the bimetal coil and mercury switch. Older units have a set of

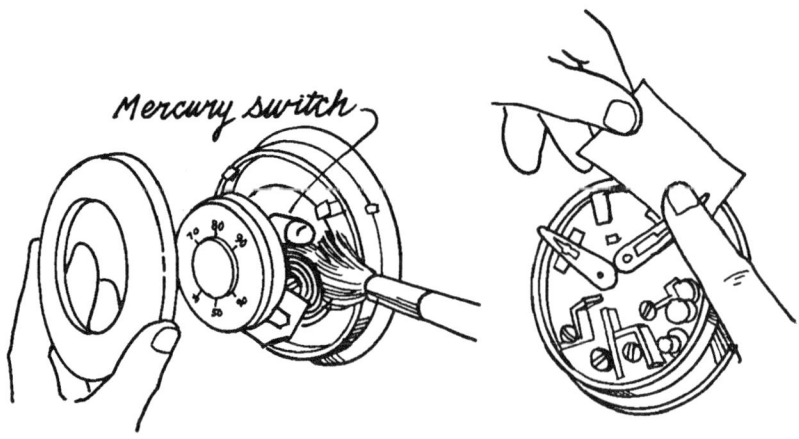

Mercury switch

Remove cover and clean once a year.
Dust off bimetal coil.
Blow dust from all surfaces.

Remove thermostat from base and clean switch contacts with paper.

contacts that open and close to regulate the heat. With the cover off (thermostats use 24 volts so it's safe to touch the wires), blow out any dust that has accumulated inside the unit. Also check that the thermostat is level, which is necessary in order for it to work properly.

Turn the heat up and as you move the thermostat lever, watch for a spark inside the unit. It should come from the mercury switch (which looks like a small vial) or from a set of contact points (located on small arms). If the spark comes from the mercury switch, you don't have to clean it because it's sealed. If the spark comes from contacts, turn the thermostat all the way down (50 degrees) to open the contact points and place a clean sheet of paper between them. Then turn the thermostat up (90 degrees) to close the contacts on the paper. Move the paper back and forth between the contacts to clean them. Turn the thermostat down and remove the paper.

If the thermostat has small levers protruding from the back that are used to control the heating/cooling cycle and the fan, you should clean their contacts. The main body of the thermostat is held to the base with a couple of screws. Just remove them and pull the thermostat body off its base. Then slip a piece of paper between the contacts and work the paper back and forth to clean them.

Round thermostats have leveling marks on the top and bottom. These marks should be aligned. Use a carpenter's level or hold a weighted string in front of the thermostat and align the marks by sight along the string. You can level rectangular thermostats by placing the level on one edge. If the thermostat is not level, loosen the mounting screws and level the unit; then retighten the screws.

TRASH COMPACTOR

To keep a garbage compactor running efficiently, make sure that it's clean and loaded properly. Load bulky trash, bottles, and cans in the center so that they're not caught between the compacting rammer and the drawer.

The interior rammer and compacting mechanism are not accessible and require no service. You can extend the life of your compactor by keeping the inside clean of garbage spills and other debris that may fall out of the garbage bag. Liquids that leak out can be corrosive and promote rusting of the cabinet. These spills will eventually produce unpleasant odors.

Most units have a pull-out drawer (similar to a file cabinet) that runs on tracks. The bag holder can be removed from this assembly for cleaning. The whole drawer unit will also come out of the compactor to allow full access to the inside. Pull the drawer all the way out of the compactor and then lift up on the end. Then lift the drawer assembly out of the roller tracks and place it on a layer of newspapers, because the bottom may be wet with liquid that has leaked from the trash bag compartment.

Clean the inside of the cabinet with hot soapy water. Wear gloves and be careful since there may be glass particles in the bottom of the compactor or on the face of the rammer, which is located in

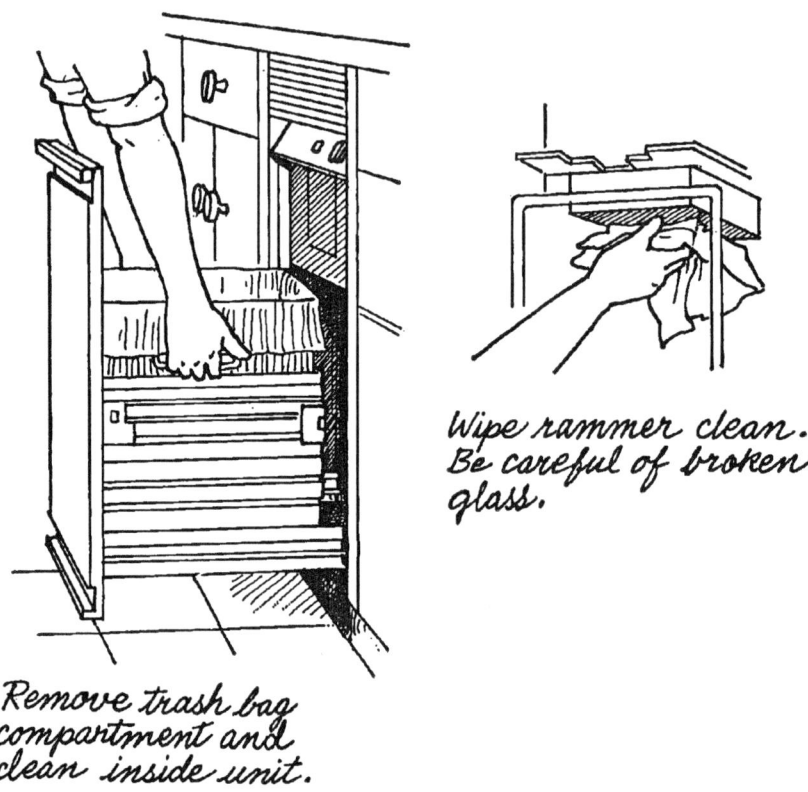

Wipe rammer clean. Be careful of broken glass.

Remove trash bag compartment and clean inside unit.

the top of the unit. Also watch out for glass when cleaning the bottom of the drawer assembly.

Give your compactor a complete cleaning **at least twice a year.** After removing a filled garbage bag and before installing a new one, clean the interior and exterior surfaces of the bag compartment with warm sudsy water and a damp cloth.

VACUUM CLEANER, Canister

A canister-type vacuum has its motor located in the top or bottom half of the canister. The motor spins a fan that draws air through the unit. Suction is created in the hose assembly, which draws in dirt that is trapped by a filter and ends up in the canister.

The motor is sealed and doesn't require regular maintenance. However you can extend the life of your vacuum by changing its filters **on a regular basis.** Clogged filters restrict the air flow through the fan, causing the unit to be inefficient and putting excessive strain on the motor, which in turn shortens its life.

Change the filter bag as soon as you notice that there is a reduction in suction at the end of the hose. This could be caused by a clogged hose, so check it out before you open the vacuum. If there's an obstruction in the hose, turn off the vacuum, unplug it from the wall, and remove the hose from the unit. Wiggle the hose to shake loose the obstruction. If that doesn't clear the hose, use a dowel or broom pushed into the hose to dislodge the blockage.

Most manufacturers recommend that you change the filter bag when it is full. Unplug the unit before you open it to check the filter. If you are temporarily out of replacement bags, you can empty and reuse one, but don't do this too frequently. The filter paper which makes up the bag becomes clogged with dirt and restricts the flow of air through it, which causes a reduction in suction. Of course, if your vacuum has a reusable cloth bag, empty it and shake the bag clean.

Some canister vacuums have a secondary filter covering the motor fan intake. It prevents dirt that may get past the filter bag from clogging the motor. This filter should be changed **whenever it looks dirty.** Use only the size and type of replaceable filter that's suggested by the manufacturer and install it properly. Check that the gasket between the filter and the canister casing is secure before you replace the top.

Store the vacuum with the hose removed from it. Gently coil the hose and store it separately. This prevents the hose from kinking and wearing out at the top elbow where it's attached to the cleaning head.

VACUUM CLEANER, Tank

A tank-type vacuum operates basically in the same way as the canister model but it's shaped differently. Tank-type vacuums are long and narrow, with the suction hose coming out of the end. The dirt is collected in a filter bag inside the unit directly behind the hose. The motor is located at the other end.

Tank-type vacuums operate exactly the same as canister units but generally have a smaller capacity dust bag. *(See the entry for "Vacuum Cleaner, Canister," page 95.)*

VACUUM CLEANER, Upright

Upright vacuums have their motor and fan in the base of the machine and collect dust and dirt in a large bag located under the handle. The motor of this type of vacuum is not easily serviced without the proper tools, but the beater brush assembly and drive belt are readily accessible.

To allow an upright vacuum to operate at peak efficiency, empty the dust bag when it is half full. *After the first year of service and every six months thereafter,* check that the beater bar and its brushes are turning. It's located at the front of the unit.

After several years of use the belt connecting the beater bar and the motor shaft may stretch and loosen. A loose belt will slip and cause the beater bar to stop rotating when it comes in contact with the carpet.

To replace a loose belt, unplug the unit and turn it over. The beater bar drive belt is located in the base of the unit under a cover plate. Remove the cover plate to expose the belt. Slip the belt off the motor shaft. You have to remove the beater bar from the vacuum so that you can slip the belt off the bar. The beater bar will snap out of its mounting bracket; if you have trouble removing it, look in the owner's manual for directions. Depending on the model, you may have to remove several retaining screws. Take the beater bar out of the vacuum and remove the belt.

Slide the new belt over the beater bar and install the bar in the vacuum. The belt must make a 90-degree twist as it runs from the beater bar to the motor shaft and proper alignment is important. There is an arrow cast in the vacuum base that shows the rotation of the belt. Twist the belt so that the part coming off the top of the beater bar (the side toward the vacuum) is closest to this arrow. Then stretch the belt back to the motor shaft and slip it into the belt groove. Reinstall the belt cover.

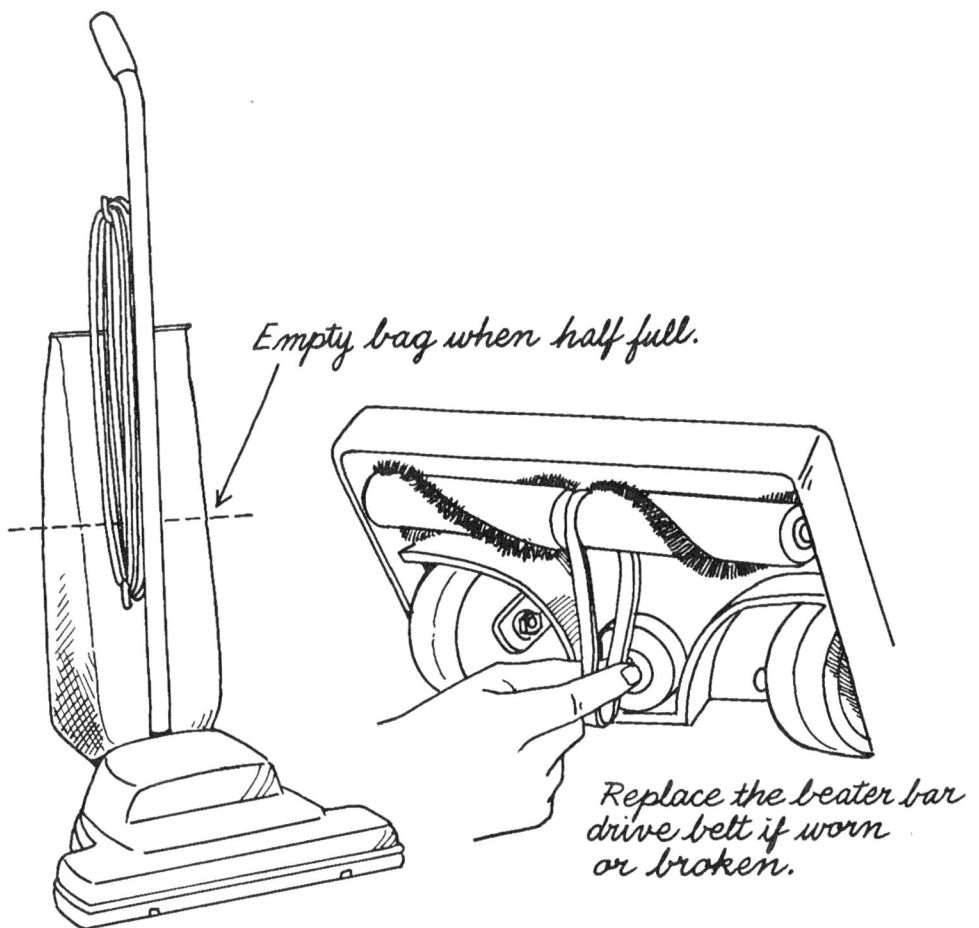

Empty bag when half full.

Replace the beater bar drive belt if worn or broken.

VIDEO CAMERA or CAMCORDER

A video camera is a cross between a camera and a videotape recorder. The lens should be cared for like a fine camera lens *(see the entry for "Camera, 35mm," on page 19, for similar maintenance tips).* The tape recorder end should be cared for like a videotape recorder *(see the entry for "Video Cassette Recorder," page 98).*

Video cameras also contain rechargeable batteries, which should be fully charged **before you store the camera for extended periods of time.** If the battery pack is removable, take it out of the camera and store it separately. Keep the lens cap in place and the power switch off when the camera is not in use.

VIDEO CASSETTE RECORDER

A video cassette recorder or VCR is a very complex machine. Like any electronic device that uses a magnetic tape to store information, the record and playback heads can accumulate oxide deposits from the tape. These deposits cause many problems, like a snowy picture or distorted audio.

Other VCR problems, such as a wavy or misaligned picture, can be caused by poor tracking. You can clean the VCR heads to correct the snowy picture but you will have to send the machine to be serviced by a trained technician if it needs realignment.

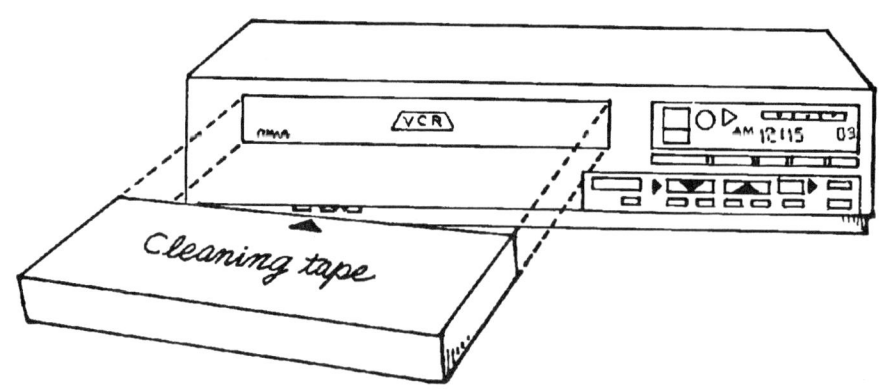

Each VCR manufacturer recommends a head cleaning schedule for its particular machine because the procedure can be abrasive to the play/record heads. Follow the manufacturer's recommendations. Some suggest using a head cleaner after every 500 hours of use; some specify a monthly cleaning; others don't recommend home cleaning at all.

It's likely the manufacturer will recommend a particular type of cleaning kit. There are spray head cleaners and head cleaning cassettes. Purchase and use the type that is recommended by the manufacturer of your VCR. If you have a new unit, check the warranty to see if any maintenance you perform will violate the warranty.

Generally, how often you clean your VCR's heads depends on how you use the machine. If you play rental tapes on a regular basis, you may have to clean the heads frequently because they are usually worn and deposit more oxide on the heads and transport parts than new tapes.

An easy-to-follow cleaning schedule is to clean the heads whenever you notice deterioration in the picture or sound, or before you record any special event. Unless your VCR owner's manual recommends otherwise, clean the heads only when they need it.

If you are a heavy tape user, you can also extend the life of the transport motor in your VCR by purchasing a rewind unit. Rewind the tapes in this inexpensive device ($30) and save wear and tear on your expensive VCR.

Heavy use will increase your maintenance. A *yearly cleaning and realignment* by a professional will assure top performance.

Spray cleaning agent into tape cartridge before each use.

WATER BED

Needless to say, a water bed contains water—with both positive and negative consequences. Although it provides a comfortable bed for sleeping, water left stagnant for any length of time is a good breeding ground for the growth of algae and unpleasant odors. To prevent this from developing inside a water bed, use an algicid additive **every six months.** These conditioners come in either tablet or liquid form and are available where water beds are sold.

To add a conditioner, unzip the mattress and open the cap. Use one tablet per tube in a soft-tube water bed. Add a liquid or several tablets to a bladder-type water bed according to the capacity of the bed. The manufacturer suggests the correct number of tablets to use on the package for different size beds.

WATER HEATER

Water that enters a hot-water heater has mineral deposits that settle in the bottom of the tank. You can increase the life and efficiency of your water heater by draining the sediment from the bottom **every other month.**

Unless you have been draining an older hot-water heater on a regular basis, starting to drain it now can cause some problems. If it's more than 5 years old, there already is a buildup of sediment that may clog the drain and cause it to leak. The drain valve on the water heater can be replaced (replacement spigots are available in hardware stores), but the tank must be drained of water.

Newer units can be safely drained since there is no sediment buildup. Connect a garden hose to the drain spigot and lead it to a floor drain. You can drain the tank into a sink, but all the water will not run out because the hose will be held higher than the bottom of the tank. (Since you only have to drain the water and the bottom of the tank to flush out the sediment, that's all right.)

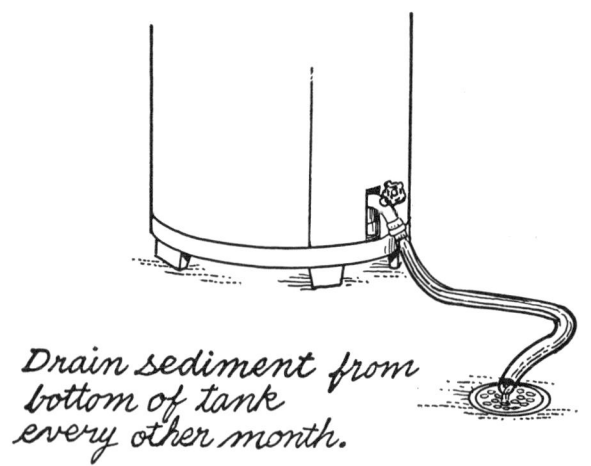

Drain sediment from bottom of tank every other month.

100

Turn the water heater off for a couple of hours before you drain it in order to allow the water to cool. If you need hot water and can't shut off the unit, be very careful because the water that runs through the hose will be very hot. Open the drain valve fully and allow the water to flow for a minute or so, or until the water draining from the hose looks clean; then close the valve. You can drain the water into a bucket, but be very careful with the hot water.

You can lengthen the life of the unit and conserve energy by setting the temperature of the thermostat on the side of the unit to no more than 140 degrees. The only appliance that requires very hot water is the dishwasher, and most will run effectively with 130- to 140-degree water.

WATER SOFTENER

A water softener is a water treatment device that removes mineral deposits that cause water to be classified as "hard." The minerals in hard water induce all sorts of problems with the plumbing and make washing more difficult. Even though water softeners are rather complicated, they are designed to run trouble-free, and for the most part, they do.

Most softeners develop problems in the brine tank and its related machinery. The water softener must dissolve salt into a brine solution and use the solution in the process of removing the mineral deposits. If your water softener is located in a warm area, condensation inside the brine tank (the large container holding the salt) can form hard salt deposits that will prevent the salt crystals, pellets or blocks from dissolving properly. When you fill the salt tank, look inside before you pour in the new salt and check for a buildup of hard salt. Break up this hard layer or chunks that have formed on the sides of the chamber. This will assure that your softener will receive the proper brine solution when the unit is recharging.

If there has been a change in the number of people living in your house, such as one of the kids being away at school, there will be a decrease in the total household water consumption. Since the softener is set to recycle more soft water than is needed, it should be reset for the correct amount.

The softener is rated according to its capacity to remove so many grains of hardness, and that capacity is specified on the unit. For example, if the water contains 10 grains of hardness per gallon and your softener can remove 13,000 grains of hardness before it must recycle, it can process about 1,300 gallons of water before it must be recharged. If there are 5 people in a household and each of them uses an average of about 50 gallons of water a day (the national average), then your softener should be set to recharge every 4 to 5 days. Recharging sooner wastes salt.

If there is a change in your water consumption, reset the recycling period. Check the owner's manual for specific instructions or ask the service technician who delivers salt to do it during his next visit.

WEATHERSTRIPPING, Spring metal

You can extend the useful life of spring metal weatherstripping almost indefinitely with a little timely maintenance.

At least once a year in the fall, inspect the weatherstripping. Look for loose nails or staples that secure the weatherstripping to the door or window jamb (side post). If they are loose, refasten them promptly. Once the spring metal gets bent out of shape, it is very difficult to straighten it out.

Use a putty knife to pry the weatherstripping away from the jamb. Bend it a little and check the fit of the door or window. You want a tight fit, but if the weatherstripping is bent too far out, the friction between the door and metal may prevent the door or window from closing.

Don't paint any kind of weatherstripping because a buildup of paint breaks down its air-sealing ability.

WICKER

Wicker furniture can last for generations if given basic care. Since the term "wicker" is used to describe furniture that can be made out of several reed types, you should determine what your furniture is made from.

Sea grass, rush, or fiber that is twisted paper wicker should be cleaned with a sponge or cloth dampened in water and a mild detergent. It should NOT be soaked with water. To maintain willow, cane or rattan, use soapy water on a brush or cloth, then dry thoroughly.

Before washing any furniture, remove dust and dirt from grooves and between the fibers of the wicker with the soft brush attachment of a vacuum cleaner.

If a piece of wicker unravels, use a drop of wood glue and push the piece back into place. Use masking tape to secure it while the glue dries.

WINDOW SHADE

To keep a window shade rolling up and down properly, make a periodic check of its bracket mechanism. Remove the shade from its brackets and look for signs of dirt or dust in the mechanism. Hold the shade on end and tap it gently to dislodge anything that's settled inside, then blow out the dirt. Apply a household oil to lubricate the mechanism. Apply the oil lightly. Over-oiling will attract dust and cause the bracket to eventually gum up.

With this routine maintenance *two times a year* you'll never have a shade that won't stay rolled down or one that's difficult to pull up and stay in place.

WINDOWS

Whereas new windows are maintenance-free, except for washing, old windows require a little more attention.

At least once a year or whenever the window sash weight pulleys squeak, squirt a spray of lubricating oil on the shafts. They are located at the top of the window jamb where the rope enters the jamb. The lower sash must be closed to expose the pulleys but the upper sash has to be open to get to them. To help quiet squeaky windows, use the extension straw of the spray oilcan to direct the oil into the center of the pulley. The oil prevents the rope pulley from wearing out, allowing the wheels that the rope runs over to turn rather than stick.

Older windows that have been painted many times tend to stick shut and become difficult to operate. Whenever you paint, take extra time to make sure that you don't paint the windows shut. As you finish painting each window, move the sashes up and down several times to break up the paint bond between the sash and jamb. Then come back in an hour or so—before the paint dries hard —and move the windows again. If the heat or air conditioning is on, open and close the windows several times before the paint sets. The next day, open and close the windows again to make sure that the new paint is not causing the windows to stick. If they stick a little, run a putty knife along the joint between the sash and jamb. This is much easier to do soon after you paint, since the paint has not fully cured.

To lubricate old windows so they'll slide more easily, use a silicone stick in the grooves of the sides of the window.

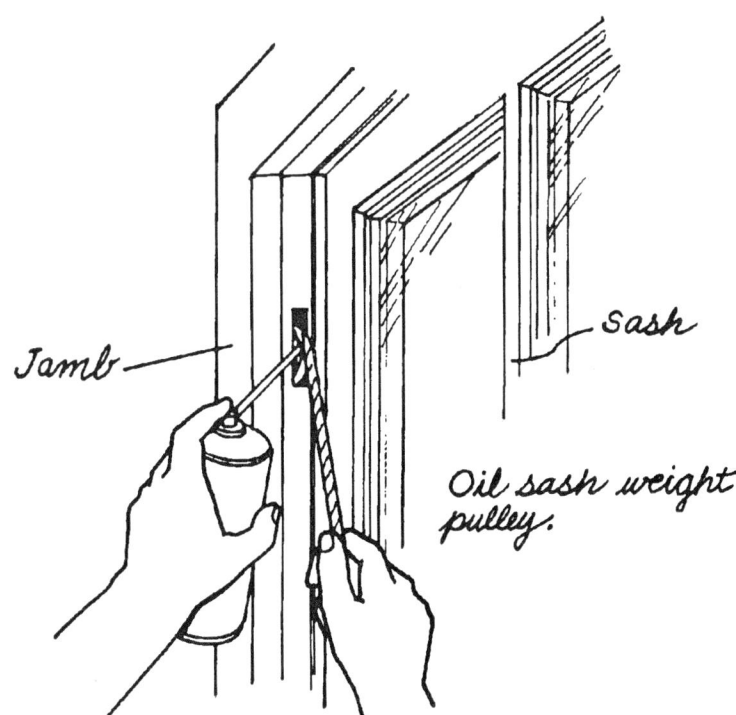

Jamb

Sash

Oil sash weight pulley.

WOOD STOVE, Catalytic

Many newer wood stoves are equipped with a ceramic catalytic element that burns the gases and particles contained in the smoke. These stoves are very efficient but do require extra maintenance. Besides some special care for the catalytic converter, the maintenance for this type of stove is the same as for any other stove. This section deals specifically with the maintenance of the catalytic converter; the following entry covers general wood stove maintenance.

Under normal operating conditions the ceramic element should last several seasons. Inspect it for cracks and missing sections **at least once a year.** One indication that the element is no longer functioning properly is a change in the rate of creosote buildup in your chimney.

The catalytic element is usually located in the upper portion of the stove near the chimney collar. Some stoves have the element in the back. Check your owner's manual for the exact location for your particular model of stove.

Follow the manufacturer's directions to disassemble the compartment holding the catalytic combuster element. Be careful working around the element because some are contained in a compartment lined with a refractory material that is very delicate. Use your shop vacuum to remove carefully all deposits of fly ash and creosote that have accumulated on top of the catalytic element.

The small honeycomb passages of the ceramic catalytic element can also become blocked by fly ash, and if you operate the stove at a low temperature it may become choked with creosote deposits. Clear these passages with a thin wire, but be careful not to damage or scratch the element.

If the element is cracked or missing sections of the honeycomb, replace it. Depending on how you

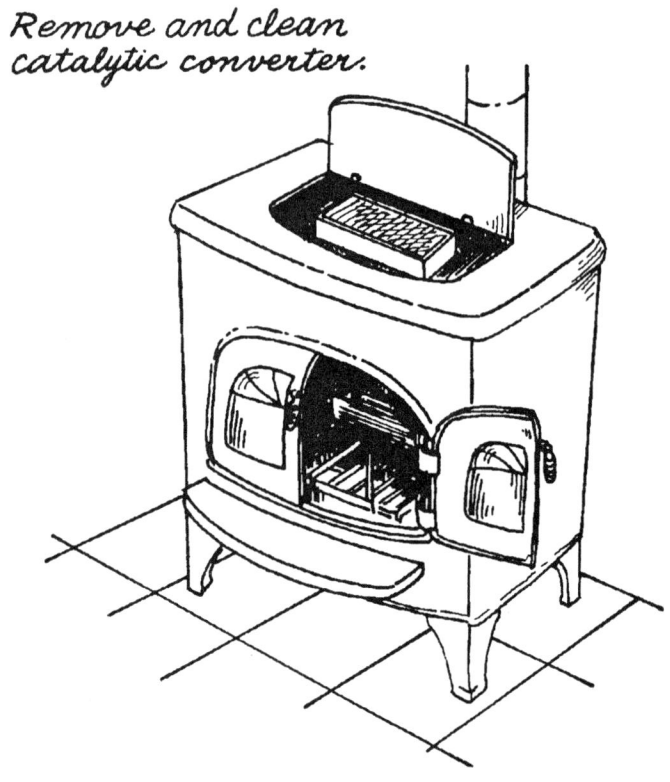

Remove and clean catalytic converter.

operate your stove, the element should last 2 to 5 years, but it will eventually fail. Your stove will not operate efficiently and will pollute the air without this element.

Reassemble the stove and as you do, check the gaskets sealing the parts around the catalytic chamber (if your stove is so equipped). If they look burnt, replace them. *(See also the entry for "Wood Stove, Non-catalytic.")*

WOOD STOVE, Non-catalytic

Wood stoves have few moving parts but they do require quite a bit of care to keep them running safely, efficiently, and longer.

At the top of the maintenance list is keeping the chimney clean. Unless you have a one-story house, this dirty job is best left to a qualified chimney sweep.

Once a year, at the end of the heating season, you should perform routine cleaning and touch-ups to the stove. First on the list is to clean away all ash and half-burnt pieces of wood that collect moisture during the summer and promote rust. When the stove is cold and the fire is out (check for live embers), sweep or vacuum up as much of the ash as possible.

Newer airtight stoves have air passages that can become clogged. Remove as many of the stove's internal parts as possible and then use the crevice tool of a vacuum to remove ashes from the tight areas inside the stove.

Next, check the stove gaskets on the doors or top griddle. These gaskets, which prevent air infiltration, become compressed over time and do not form an airtight seal. **After several seasons of use,** the gaskets should be replaced. The manufacturer of your stove most likely sells a gasket replacement kit for your particular model. You can also purchase stove gasket material by the foot, along with a tube of gasket cement from any store that sells wood stoves.

To replace a gasket on the grille or doors of a stove, first pull out the old gasket material and scrape away any dried cement from the groove.

Apply a thin bead of new gasket cement to the groove and push the gasket into the groove as far as it will go. Close the door to seat the gasket, then open the door and wipe up the excess cement that may have squeezed out of the groove.

Black cast-iron stoves should be wiped down with a damp rag, to remove any dirt and dust, and thoroughly dried. Apply stove polish to keep the stove from developing surface rust during the summer lay-up.

To clean an enameled stove, wipe off any dirt or soot with a half vinegar and half water solution. Chipped paint should be repaired with a touch-up kit sold by the stove manufacturer. *(See the entry for "Stove Pipe," page 85, for more maintenance suggestions.)*

Remove ash with vacuum's crevice tool.